Leadership

Where Else Can We Go?

Leadership

Where Else Can We Go?

Edited by Morgan W. McCall, Jr.
and Michael M. Lombardo

Duke University Press   Durham, N.C.   1978

2   3   4   5   6   7   8   9

*to the many researchers and practitioners
who have grappled with the issues of leadership,*

and to Liz and Susan

Contents

Contributors

Jeffrey Pfeffer received his Ph.D. in Organizational Behavior from Stanford University. He has written about boards of directors and political processes in organizations and is actively studying power, decision making, environmental effects on organizations, and organization structure. He is presently Associate Professor of Organizational Behavior–Industrial Relations in the School of Business Administration and Associate Research Sociologist in the Institute of Industrial Relations, University of California at Berkeley.

Craig Lundberg is currently Chairman of the Department of Management and Professor of Business Administration at Oregon State University. An active consultant and researcher, his interests include management training and development, decision making, organizational roles, and executive styles.

Author of *The Social Psychology of Organizing* and coauthor of *Managerial Behavior, Performance, and Effectiveness,* **Karl Weick** is Professor of Psychology and Organizational Behavior at Cornell University. His diverse interests include group processes, organizational change, structure and theory, research methods in the social sciences, attitude change, cognition, equity, and dissonance theory. Currently he has editorial responsibilities with *Organizational Behavior and Human Performance, Administrative Science Quarterly,* and *Contemporary Psychology.*

Louis R. Pondy received his Ph.D. in Industrial Administration from Carnegie-Mellon University. He has written about organizational conflict, resource allocation, and health systems. His current interests include application of general systems theory concepts to organizational design and management problems in the public sector. He is Professor of Organizational Behavior, University of Illinois–Urbana.

Managerial strategy and behavior, organization development, and interrelations of organizational technologies and behavior are the special interests of **Peter B. Vaill.** Vaill, Dean of the School of Government and Business Administration and Professor of Management Science at George Washington University, has been active in organizational consulting and management training.

Ian I. Mitroff received his Ph.D. in Engineering Science from the University of California at Berkeley. He has written about the interface between people and technology, designing information systems for the future, and systems theory. He is currently interested in decision making under uncertainty, organizational problem solving, and training people to think dialectically. He is presently Professor of Business, Information Science, and Sociology in the Graduate School of Business, University of Pittsburgh.

About the editors

Morgan W. McCall, Jr., Ph.D., a research psychologist who joined the Center in 1974, is responsible for research on issues in leadership. He has had experience as an organizational consultant, has taught organizational behavior, and has written several publications. His research and writing have centered on aspects of leadership such as leader-system relationships, managerial information and feedback, assessment centers, and research methodologies. He is currently involved in multiyear studies of leader-system relationships, managerial feedback, and leadership effectiveness.

Michael M. Lombardo, Ed.D., joined the Center staff in 1974 and currently oversees the completion and distribution of Center publications. Dr. Lombardo teaches educational administration at the University of North Carolina at Greensboro, where he holds an adjunct appointment, and has done research and writing on educational simulations and the relationship of schools and juvenile delinquency. He is also involved in a multiyear study of leader-system relationships and a national curriculum project to develop educational games for the classroom.

Preface

Recently I read a journal report by a well-known experimental psychologist in which he reviewed a number of animal experiments and their results. His report ended with the sentence: "At this point, however, the discussion begins to go beyond the boundaries set by well-established data." That statement justified his termination of the discourse. It could just as well serve to begin the discourse that you will find between the covers of this book.

Sometimes I feel that all discussions in social science should begin, at least implicitly, with such an introduction. A growing number of writers and presenters of conference papers (I attend a staggering number of conferences) seem to feel that in their pursuit of New Worlds of Knowledge social scientists usually cast off from pieces of flotsam and jetsam rather than from a solid dock, and navigate by more or less randomly appearing spots before their eyes as much as by clear, fixed stars. Even many of those who would not accept this assessment as applied to their own work would still agree that it seems to fit well enough the work of others.

It is no secret that dissatisfaction with methods and with results is rampant among social scientists, across a wide spectrum of content areas. Too many sightings of solid land in the last twenty-five years have turned out to be false discoveries; there is a feeling of disillusionment and an urge to throw the captain overboard. No captains can be found—only a yellowed document spelling out the canons of experimental science, and hardly anyone (at least, hardly anyone still writing or showing up at conferences) is willing to throw this overboard completely. But there is earnest debate about which parts of this document have served us poorly and deserve to be revised, and which parts still provide a sine qua non for the investigative enterprise.

This conference, at least as I experienced it, was an effort to consider some of these revisions, as they might affect the effort to learn something important about leadership. Participants agreed that we are all in the same boat (i.e., things are not going very well) but suggested a variety of navigational improvements. Some may even have been suggesting that while we debated navigation the ship was sinking; the important question may be whether or not a lifeboat can be found.

Perhaps I have carried this metaphor too far. Still, it should convey to the reader the idea that the tone of the presentations at this conference was rather different from the more typical scientific discussion of subjects chosen, methods applied, and conclusions drawn. A major theme, dominant in setting the tone, was the assertion that we need to *rediscover the phenomena* of leadership; the pursuit of rigor and precision has led to an over-emphasis on techniques at the expense of knowing what is going on in a direct, human way. As a result, we have masses of "find-ings" that no one seems able to pull together—they simply float around in the literature, providing nothing from which one can push off to anywhere. Much of the discussion had to do with suggesting ways in which people might study leadership and get results that make better contact with the problems and challenges faced by real leaders and managers.

Psychology, and perhaps related disciplines, is in for a period of "unfreezing" of its attachment to the alleged norms of physical science. I do not know of any book other than this one that has so single-minded a devotion to this goal as it relates to the study of leadership.

James Lester
Office of Naval Research

Acknowledgments

The editors wish to give special thanks to the Center for Creative Leadership, Greensboro, North Carolina, which made possible the conference from which this book resulted.

Among the many people we would like to thank are Joanne Ferguson and Kathy Schneider for the coordination of the project, Lon Murdick for media support, Frank Freeman and Norma Kay for technical assistance, and those persons who provided constructive advice during the various stages of writing, especially Larry Cummings of the University of Wisconsin.

Finally, a special note of gratitude to Zella Stiles, who tirelessly typed, edited, and worried over innumerable drafts of the manuscript.

Morgan W. McCall, Jr.
Michael M. Lombardo

November 1, 1976
Greensboro, North Carolina

Leadership

Where Else Can We Go?

1. Leadership

Michael M. Lombardo
and Morgan W. McCall, Jr.

Leadership is one of the most magnetic words in the English language. Mention it, and a perceptible aura of excitement, almost mystical in nature, appears. Macbeth, Marie Antoinette, Hannibal, Lincoln, Caesar—such names are electric. The fascination with leaders is so great that *Time* magazine (July 15, 1974) devoted most of an issue to American leaders and the phenomenon of leadership.

There is a universal interest in leaders and what makes them tick. How did Martin Luther King make blacks believe they could achieve equality? How did Robert E. Lee win all those battles? How did Henry Ford produce a corporate giant from a Tin Lizzie? Anyone looking for the answers in leadership research invites disappointment from two sources. First, the answers are clearly not to be found. Second, if leadership is bright orange, leadership research is slate gray.

Why should anyone want to read another book about leadership? Already besieged by literally thousands of articles, books, pamphlets, audio tapes, and films, students of leadership—academics and practitioners alike—have no doubt discovered three things: (1) the number of unintegrated models, theories, prescriptions, and conceptual schemes of leadership is mind-boggling; (2) much of the literature is fragmentary, trivial, unrealistic, or dull; and (3) the research results are characterized by Type III errors (solving the wrong problem precisely) and by contradictions.

A sense of frustration

Such feelings are not recent in origin. Leadership research, as an area of empirical interest, can be traced to 1939 when Lewin,

Lippitt, and White's now classic study appeared. As early as 1959 Bennis summarized the progress to date:

> Of all the hazy and confounding areas in social psychology, leadership theory undoubtedly contends for top nomination. And, ironically, probably more has been written and less known about leadership than about any other topic in the behavioral sciences. Always, it seems, the concept of leadership eludes us or turns up in another form to taunt us again with its slipperiness and complexity. So we have invented an endless proliferation of terms to deal with it . . . and still the concept is not sufficiently defined. As we survey the path leadership theory has taken, we spot the wreckage of "trait theory," the "great man" theory, and the "situationist critique," leadership styles, functional leadership, and finally, leaderless leadership; to say nothing of bureaucratic leadership, charismatic leadership, democratic-autocratic-laissez-faire leadership, group-centered leadership, reality-centered leadership, leadership by objective, and so on. The dialectic and reversals of emphases in this area very nearly rival the tortuous twists and turns of child-rearing practices, and one can paraphrase Gertrude Stein by saying, "a leader is a follower is a leader."
>
> The lack of consensus in this whole area of leadership and authority cannot be blamed on a reluctance by social scientists to engage in empirical research on projects related to these topics. In fact, the problem is not so much that there is little evidence, but that the mountain of evidence which is available appears to be so contradictory, and some of the theorists have radically modified their own points of view in the course of their writings on these subjects. [pp. 259–260]

Interestingly, Bennis' comment was published before the advent and popularity of the LPC and Fiedler's contingency model, before the various "transactional" and "interpersonal accommodation" models, before the infiltration of path-goal models into the leadership arena, and relatively early in the empirical history of "initiating structure" and "consideration."

More recently, Stogdill undertook the gargantuan task of bringing the state of the art up-to-date. In 1974 he published

The Handbook of Leadership, a review and analysis of more than three thousand books and articles on leadership. Anyone with hopes of finding answers to the leadership enigma in this volume need look no farther than the first page of the preface, where Stogdill tartly comments:

> Four decades of research on leadership have produced a bewildering mass of findings. Numerous surveys of special problems have been published, but they seldom include all the studies available on a topic. It is difficult to know what, if anything, has been convincingly demonstrated by replicated research. *The endless accumulation of empirical data has not produced an integrated understanding of leadership.* [p. vii; italics added]

This painful state of affairs in the field of leadership is not without consequences. Practitioners have been frustrated by premature applications of behavioral science knowledge (e.g., human relations, sensitivity training), by the triviality of some of the research (e.g., seating position influences on the emergence of leadership in a small group), and by the proliferation of jargon (e.g., "the zero order correlations, in each moderated group, were compared to comparable second order partials between the given leader scale and dependent variables, holding the other two leader behavior variables constant").

As a result, the potential contribution of research on leadership to actual leadership in organizations has been and continues to be reduced. A central aim of this research—to help practitioners become more effective leaders—depends to a great extent on training them in various skills and modes of behavior; and the results of studies on training effects are not encouraging. There is little doubt that training produces temporary changes in those undergoing it, but there is little evidence of long-term effects (Miner, 1965).

Campbell, Dunnette, Lawler, and Weick (1970) and Gibb (1974, pp. 155–177) have questioned the assumptions underlying many training programs that traditionally focus on human relations, i.e., on attitudinal, internal sorts of changes. Attitudes such as "consideration" or employee-centeredness are taught, but there is almost no evidence that such attitudes are related to performance (Korman, 1968; Campbell et al., 1970). Even if they are related, the causal arrow could point either way, for it makes as much sense to say that performance leads to considerate attitudes as that considerate attitudes lead to performance. Recent studies (Porter & Lawler, 1968; Schwab & Cummings, 1970; Sheridan & Slocum, 1975) indicate that under different conditions the arrow does point both ways.

This example points up the central dilemma in applying leadership research to leadership in organizations. It is fantasy to expect a simple, linear relationship between attitudes and performance (Fisher, 1959, said the relationship looked like "a twisted pear"); it is even more fanciful to expect that other internal and external criteria (job attitudes and turnover, for example; Kraut, 1975) relate in some simple fashion.

Practitioners often chide researchers with the blanket question, "When are you going to look at organizations as they really are?" In other words, when are you going to train us in things that have any importance for organizational goals and that reflect the variety and interrelatedness we face?

Social scientists have joined practitioners in these feelings of frustration. One researcher commented that he had been away from the field for fifteen years and felt that it has only been fifteen minutes: the vocabulary, methods, and conclusions seemed much the same. Other, more caustic critics (Perrow, 1972; Miner, 1975) have suggested that the term "leadership" has outlived its usefulness and should be scrapped. Perrow said:

> One is tempted to say that the research on leadership has left us with the clear view that things are far more complicated and "contingent" than we initially believed, and that, in fact, they are so complicated and contingent that it may not be worth our while to spit out more and more categories and qualifications. [p. 115]

Even Stogdill suggests more of what Perrow laments. He calls for a paradigm of the twenty-five experimental and six criterion variables that hold the most promise of being strongly related to leadership. In simplest form, his paradigm would require three hundred manipulations to assess the effects of the experimental variables, and Stogdill admits that most of the variables (per-

sonality and expectations, for example) are not unitary characteristics. This means that the actual range of combinations of these
variables is many times three hundred, and even three hundred
is far too great a number to have any value to practitioners. Can
anyone imagine a manager considering which variable or groups
of variables are appropriate to a particular situation? "Let's see,
I have to interact with Mary and Bill, so conditional models 83,
112, and 199 seem the way to go."

Exploring the unsaid

Enough said. Anyone can criticize, and some things are easier to
criticize than others. Criticism alone will help neither social
scientists nor practitioners. As Robert Heinlein said, "It's a hell
of a note when you can't even kill a dragon and feel lighthearted
afterwards" (1970, p. 169).

Observing leadership research from the other side of the looking glass—considering what has been left unsaid rather than what
has been said and said and said—makes it appear that there are
at least two major omissions.

One, leadership theories have traditionally been short-range and
atomistic, focusing on leader-group relations and passing over
leader-group-system relationships. Indeed, there is no such section
in Stogdill's massive review. The reductionist view of leadership
fragments reality. Leaders and their groups are embedded in
complex, often contradictory organizational systems, and to examine them outside this context ignores the richness of reality. How
workers feel about themselves and their leader is not everything
—it is only important in the context of the tasks they are performing and the varied, external demands of the organization.

Two, there is a plethora of studies describing portions of what
leaders and their subordinates say they do, could do, or should
do; but only a smattering of studies describing what they *actually*
do. Real life is complex, superficial, ambiguous, and irrational; but
if the knowledge of the behavioral sciences is to be translated into
usable guidelines for leaders, observational studies must complement the controlled conditions of the laboratory.

Current leadership theory and techniques cannot cope with
these two omissions, but knowing from which point to break away

is not the same as knowing where to go. It was with this goal in mind—"Where else can we go?"—that a different kind of conference on leadership was conceived at the Center for Creative Leadership, Greensboro, North Carolina. What would happen if a group of social scientists, with solid reputations for creative thinking, but *not* noted primarily for their work on leadership, were asked to deal with the question: "Leadership: Where Else Can We Go?" What if such people were unfettered by a requirement for formal papers, challenged to be irreverent and go out on a limb, and surrounded by a diverse audience of trainers, students, academics, and practitioners? On June 30–July 1, 1975, we found out. This book is an attempt to share that experience with you.

The following social scientists accepted invitations to present their ideas and run workshops at the conference:

Jeffrey Pfeffer, Associate Professor, School of Business Administration, and Associate Research Sociologist in the Institute of Industrial Relations, University of California, Berkeley;

Karl Weick, Professor of Psychology and Organizational Behavior, Cornell University;

Ian Mitroff, Professor of Business, Information Science, and Sociology in the Graduate School of Business, University of Pittsburgh;

Craig Lundberg, Chairman, Department of Management, and Professor of Business Administration, School of Business, Oregon State University;

Louis Pondy, Professor of Business Administration, University of Illinois; and

Peter Vaill, Dean of the School of Government and Business Administration and Professor of Management Science, George Washington University.

The themes that emerged from the conference will be analyzed in detail in Chapter 9, "Where Else Can We Go?" As a foreshadowing, two broad, often antithetical themes recurred throughout the proceedings.

Systems—"We need to understand the reality around us—the reality of the whole. The best social science reporting comes from journalism, not from researchers. Norman Mailer's *Of a Fire on the Moon* is an excellent example of someone's immersing himself in and trying to understand a large complex system rather than fragmenting it." (Peter Vaill)

Variety—"We should be documenting the variety in leadership rather than the uniformity. With uniformity, we get caught up in definitions—for example, leadership as a social influence; such categories are not useful." (Louis Pondy)

Putting these two themes together was the principal aim of the conference. If leaders face an infinite variety of situations and act in an infinite variety of ways, how can this hodgepodge of inputs and outputs be integrated into a systems concept? Weick joined these themes by noting that a leader has to be as complicated as the environment he or she is up against to control and regulate that environment. He combined the opposites of variety and system into what he called a medium—a sensitive leader who can pick up nuances and subtleties from the environment and has the skill to interrelate and act on these elements.

To study these mediums, people who are externally constrained so as to register variety, and internally constrained so as to act systematically, researchers will have to become "unstatistical naturalists" and "differentiating generalists" able to get into a system and see what is going on.

Three phases emerged during the conference in an attempt to examine the complex and contradictory relationships of leaders, groups, systems, macro and micro forces—the mosaic of organizations.

The first phase was a data-based overview of leadership research to assess what is known about leadership effectiveness. Based on his review of the literature and personal research, Pfeffer questioned whether leadership matters as much as we think it does. Leaders are embedded in complex social systems where power is shared, organizational policy limits their efforts, the expectations of others may control them, and vast forces such as the economy or natural disasters may subvert their impact. Pfeffer explained much of our thinking about leadership as attribution—the tendency of human beings to attribute outcomes to persons rather than shadowy, contextual forces outside their control. Leadership in its present sense is a myth designed to simplify events and their causation, and the myths of leadership should be separated from the analysis of leadership as a process of social influence involving innumerable organizational and environmental demands.

But how is that done? How can one capture an infinite phenomenon so it can be studied? Several of the speakers suggested specific approaches during the second phase of the conference. Weick discussed the notion of requisite variety in systems—a conceptual framework to identify and measure what leaders do, not what they have done. Trying to generate enough contingencies to explain leadership is probably hopeless, but exploring deeper levels such as Weick's leader as medium may provide some answers. Pondy paralleled Weick's concern with the deep structure of leadership by drawing analogies from the field of linguistics.

The speakers presented specific variables that illustrated deeper or neglected areas of leadership—energy level, types of information-processing, level of intuition, nondistractability, time perspective, etc. Lundberg presented six variables in need of recognition, among them the self-expectations of leaders, and leaders' uses of lieutenants to form coalitions in the hierarchy. This latter variable may help to explain delegation strategies in systems terms.

Vaill and Mitroff, during the final phase of the conference, extended the previous arguments into broad conceptual approaches and methodologies for leadership research. Vaill listed eight assumptions that permeate social science research—assumptions of questionable validity. The result of believing in these assumptions is that, "We keep going into social systems we don't know anything about, expecting to come out with some kind of document." Vaill mused that researchers who reject the eight assumptions would produce documents that look radically different from the patchwork of statistics on leadership we now have. Toward that end, he proposed forty-seven hypotheses that might describe what high-performing systems and their leaders look like.

Mitroff noted that the social sciences have attempted to use the methods of the physical sciences to explain human phenomena. To do this, people have been chopped up, and amorphous organizational dilemmas have been recast into well-structured, preformulated problems. Mitroff charged (echoing Pfeffer) that all the important problems are ill-structured, fuzzy things that researchers have yet to identify. He then presented a dialectical process of problem identification to provide a framework for leadership research.

Regardless of the direction of their arguments, the speakers converged on the two broad themes that permeated the conference—resistance to reductionistic thinking and the need to get out there and see what is going on, the ability to feel the flow and the subtle eddies of events just as the members of the system do. This sense of direction may have been best summarized when Vaill mentioned his favorite high-performing system of 1974—the University of Southern California football team that blitzed Notre Dame for fifty-five points in seventeen minutes. "What was happening was so complex and so much a product of the operation of the whole system, it is just crazy to try to come down to one leader and say, 'He pulled the trigger.'"

These essays represent *ideas* about leadership and research. While many of the contentions rest on empirical foundations, this is not a collection of studies. Their value lies not in elaboration of previous theories, or even in the presentation of polished new theories, but primarily in the modes of thinking represented by the authors.

Three of the participants (Vaill, Pondy, and Lundberg) presented papers along with their commentary. The other three spoke from notes. In this book we have attempted to integrate their written and spoken words to maintain the flavor of what went on at the conference.

Pfeffer began the conference with a data-based overview of the relation of leadership to organizational effectiveness, a review that produced dismal results. Not only is the evidence of leadership effects sketchy, but evidence of the magnitude of these effects is nonexistent. Such findings are reflected in the question that permeates the next chapter: How do we know that leadership matters?

References

Bennis, W. G. Leadership theory and administrative behavior: The problem of authority. *Administrative Science Quarterly*, 1959, **4**, 259–260.

12   1. Leadership

Campbell, J. P., Dunnette, M., Lawler, E., III, & Weick, K., Jr. *Managerial behavior, performance, and effectiveness.* New York: McGraw-Hill, 1970.

Fisher, J. The twisted pear and the prediction of behavior. *Journal of Consulting Psychology,* 1959, **23,** 400–405.

Gibb, J. R. The message from research. In J. W. Pfeiffer & J. E. Jones (Eds.), *The 1974 annual handbook for group facilitators.* La Jolla, Calif.: University Associates, 1974.

Heinlein, R. A. *Glory road.* New York: Berkeley Publishing, 1970.

Korman, A. K. The prediction of managerial performance: A review. *Personnel Psychology,* 1968, **21,** 295–322.

Kraut, A. Predicting turnover of employees from measured job attitudes. *Organizational Behavior and Human Performance,* 1975, **13,** 233–243.

Lewin, K., Lippitt, R., & White, R. K. Patterns of aggressive behavior in experimentally created "social climates." *The Journal of Social Psychology,* 1939, **10,** 271–299.

Miner, J. B. *Studies in management education.* New York: Springer, 1965.

Miner, J. B. *The uncertain future of the leadership concept: An overview.* Paper presented at the Third Leadership Symposium, Southern Illinois University at Carbondale, March 1975.

Perrow, C. *Complex organizations: A critical essay.* Glenview, Ill.: Scott, Foresman, 1972.

Porter, L. W., & Lawler, E. E. *Managerial attitudes and performance.* Homewood, Ill.: Irwin, 1968.

Schwab, D. P., & Cummings, L. L. Theories of performance and satisfaction. *Industrial Relations,* 1970, **10,** 408–430.

Sheridan, J. E., & Slocum, J. W., Jr. The direction of the causal relationship between job satisfaction and work performance. *Organizational Behavior and Human Performance,* 1975, **14,** 159–173.

Stogdill, R. M. *Handbook of leadership.* New York: Free Press, 1974.

2. *The Ambiguity of Leadership*

Jeffrey Pfeffer

Leadership has for some time been a major, if not dominant, topic in both social and organizational psychology. Underlying much of this research has been the sometimes implicit, sometimes explicit assumption that leadership is causally related to organizational performance. Through an analysis of appropriate leadership styles, behaviors, or characteristics (depending on the theoretical perspective chosen), the argument has been made that more effective leaders can be selected or trained or, alternatively, the situation can be configured to provide for enhanced leader and, consequently, organizational effectiveness. The emphasis on leadership as a topic for research in organizational behavior has been justified by a belief that leadership was important in organizational functioning and that if theories of leadership could be developed, the selection and training of leaders would be improved, with a consequent increase in organizational effectiveness.

This essay will argue that the fundamental assumptions stated above are probably incorrect and at least deserve explicit investigation. I intend to review theory and research bearing on the following basic issues in the study of leadership: (1) the ambiguity of definitions and measurement of the concept, and the ambiguity in research findings; (2) the question of whether leadership matters—is there any evidence of leadership effects on organizational outcomes?; and (3) the issue of how leaders are selected—who attains leadership positions and what are the implications of this selection process for normative theories of

A version of this essay appeared in the *Academy of Management Review*, 2:1, 1977.

leadership selection and training? The essay concludes with some theoretical reconceptualizations of the leadership phenomenon, and with implications of this reconceptualization for theory and research on this topic. My intent is to continue the analysis of basic definitions and issues associated with the study of leadership, such as that undertaken by Kochan, Schmidt, and DeCotiis (1975).

The ambiguity of the concept

In spite of the voluminous research on leadership, the definition and the dimensions of the concept remain uncertain. As to definition, the task is to distinguish leadership from other processes of social influence. Kochan et al. (1975) distinguish leadership from authority by showing that in leadership, influence rights are voluntarily conferred. These authors distinguish leadership from power by the notion of goal compatibility, arguing that power does not require goal compatibility, merely dependence; but leadership implies some congruence between the objectives of the leader and the led. Hollander and Julian (1969) and Bavelas (1960) did not draw such sharp distinctions between leadership and other social influence processes. Indeed, one of the major points of the Hollander and Julian review was that research on leadership would progress more rapidly if the findings and concepts from social influence research were incorporated. It is fair to state that there is agreement that leadership is related to social influence and power. Whether it is a unique process depends, using the Kochan et al. definitions, on whether one can distinguish voluntary from involuntary compliance, and whether goal compatibility is a stable and meaningful concept. We can note in passing that attitudes follow, as well as precede, behaviors, and that goal statements and the meaning of action may be retrospectively inferred (Schutz, 1967; Weick, 1969).

Concepts of voluntarism and goals raise additional complexities to the definition of leadership. While there is some basic consensus on the social influence component of leadership, there is more disagreement concerning the basic dimensions of leader behavior. Some authors have argued that there are two tasks that must be accomplished in groups—the maintenance of the group and the accomplishment of some task or goal shared by the

Behavior

Jeffrey Pfeffer 15

group. These two dimensions of group maintenance and group achievement have been used by Collins and Guetzkow (1964) and by Cartwright and Zander (1960) to describe leader behavior. House (1971), in his expectancy theory-based formulation of the path goal theory of leadership, retains these two dimensions of leader behavior, writing of social and task behaviors. Halpin and Winer (1957, pp. 39–51), using factor analysis on an extensive questionnaire, uncovered four dimensions of leader behavior: consideration, initiating structure, production emphasis, and sensitivity (social awareness). Since the third and fourth factors explained relatively little variance, they were dropped, leaving the well-known factors of consideration and initiating structure. Hemphill and Coons (1957, pp. 6–38) discovered three factors: maintenance of membership character, objective attainment behavior, and group interaction facilitation.

Consideration and initiating structure can, perhaps, be seen as similar to the group maintenance and task accomplishment dimensions discussed by Cartwright and Zander. But additional ways of giving dimension to leader behavior also exist. Bowers and Seashore (1966) proposed four dimensions of leadership: support, interaction facilitation, goal emphasis, and work facilitation. Day and Hamblin (1964) analyzed leadership behavior in terms of two dimensions, one being close versus general supervision, and the other being punitive versus nonpunitive supervision. Several authors have conceptualized leadership behavior in terms of the authority and discretion that subordinates are permitted. These descriptions of leadership styles grow out of the research of Lewin, Lippitt, and White (Lippitt, 1940), in which three leadership styles—democratic, authoritarian, and laissez-faire—were identified. Heller and Yukl (1969) describe leadership behavior as being either decision centralized or participative, and Lowin (1968) reviewed several studies that examined the effects of leadership styles which varied in terms of their participativeness. Participation, or decision centralization, seems to be the currently favored dimension for describing leadership, forming the basis for Yukl's (1971) theory of leadership and for the work of Vroom and Yetton (1973). Fiedler (1967) analyzed leadership in terms of the least-preferred-coworker scale (LPC), but the meaning and behavioral attributes of this dimension of leadership remain a subject of controversy.

To add further ambiguity, not only are there a multitude of dimensions describing leadership 'behavior, but the literature assessing the effects of leadership, described by each dimension, is equivocal. Korman (1966) reviewed research on leadership effectiveness in which the dimensions of consideration and initiating structure were used, but he found relatively small and inconsistent results. Sales (1966) summarized the leadership literature that employed the authoritarian-democratic typology, with similarly pessimistic conclusions, while Lowin (1968) reviewed the literature examining the effects of participative decision making. In each case, both methodological and theoretical problems were uncovered, and the typical prescription has been that the effectiveness of leadership styles is contingent, and the various contingencies must be taken into account. Leadership style effectiveness is contingent on subordinates' personalities (Vroom, 1959) and situational characteristics (Heller & Yukl, 1969; Vroom & Yetton, 1973).

The proliferation of dimensions is, in part, a function of the methodology that has been frequently employed. Factor analysis on a large number of items describing behavior has been the commonly used procedure for uncovering leadership dimensions. This, first of all, tends to produce as many factors as the analyst decides to find. By appropriately choosing algorithms and significance levels, factor solutions can be made to vary. Even more important, the resultant factors must be named, introducing some further confusion and imprecision since the naming of the factors is, at best, a very subjective process. Some of the dimensions reviewed were empirically derived; others were constructed based on the theoretical orientation of the researcher. The relationship among the dimensions remains unclear, and there exists as yet little conclusive evidence supporting the relationship between any of the dimensions of leadership behavior and measures of organizational performance. The results are, of course, stronger when self-report or attitudinal measures of outcomes are used.

The effects of leaders

Hall (1972, p. 248) asked a basic question about leadership—is there any evidence on the magnitude of the effects of leadership? Surprisingly, he could find no research on this fundamental issue, and currently the situation is about the same. Given the resources that have been spent studying, selecting, and training leaders, one might expect that the question of whether or not leaders matter would have been explored before.

It is not necessary to have a theory predicting a relationship between a specific type of leadership behavior or style and performance in order to address the issue of the magnitude of leadership effects. Leadership effects can be ascertained by decomposing the variance in some organizational measure, by assessing the variance attributable to other possible causal factors (such as context and year), and by assessing the variance apparently associated with leadership (the effects of leadership are determined by noting the consequences of changes in occupants of leadership positions). Thus, the analysis of the effects of leadership is possible, even given the current conceptual ambiguity of the concept itself.

There are at least three reasons why it might be argued that the observed effects of leaders on organizational performance would be small. First, those obtaining leadership positions are selected and, in the process of this selection, only certain, limited styles of behavior may be chosen. Second, once in the leadership position, the discretion and behavior of the leader are constrained. And third, leaders can affect, typically, only a few of the variables that may have an impact on organizational performance.

Constraints on who is selected

At any organizational level, and certainly as one moves up the organizational hierarchy, the range in leadership attributes or behavior one is likely to find is limited. People do not attain leadership positions in a random fashion; they are selected. The literature on attraction (Berscheid & Walster, 1969) indicates that there is a tendency for persons to like those who are perceived as being similar to themselves. In decisions as critical as job promotions, when there are invariably more candidates than positions, it is likely that persons who have styles of behavior that "fit," or are similar to those already prevalent in the organization, are those selected for leadership. While there exists a large normative literature on selection, it is unfortunately the case that there are few comparative studies examining the actual promotion process. But the rationale seems persuasive that social similarity will be one dimension used in the selection of leaders. The promotion process involves a filtering of persons at each level, and at each filtering the likelihood increases that only similar behavioral patterns will be selected.

Selection of persons to leadership positions is constrained also by the internal system of influence in the organization. As Zald (1965) has noted, succession is a critical decision in organizations, and is frequently affected by political influence.

Since the selection process is affected by the system of influence, only when the distribution of power within the organization changes would the selection criteria and their outcome also be likely to change. In most instances the distribution of power within organizations is probably relatively stable (e.g., Thompson, 1967), if for no other reason than being in power affords the power holders certain advantages in maintaining their position. Then, it is likely that the selection system itself will remain stable over time, tending to select similar types of persons for leadership.

Succession to leadership positions is also affected by the environmental contingencies faced by the organization. According to the strategic contingencies theory of intraorganizational power (Hickson, Hinings, Lee, Schneck, & Pennings, 1971), power derives from the ability to cope with critical organizational uncertainties that may arise from interactions between the organization and its environment. Since power affects the succession process, and environmental contingencies affect the distribution of power, then, by extension, environmental contingencies also affect the choice of leaders. Further, as Thompson has argued, leaders are occasionally selected specifically for their capacity to deal with various organizational contingencies. To the extent that the contingencies faced by the organization remain stable, then the abilities and behaviors of those selected into leadership positions will also remain stable.

Finally, the selection of persons to leadership positions is affected by a self-selection process. Organizations have images, providing information about their individual characteristics. Also leadership roles in organizations have images, providing information about their character as well. Persons are likely to select themselves into organizations, and into roles within those organizations, based upon their preferred images. This self-selection process would tend to work, along with the process of organizational selection, to limit the range of abilities and behaviors that one would be likely to find in a given organizational role. While it is no doubt true that role incumbency shapes people's attitudes and orientations, it is also true that there is a process of anticipatory socialization, in which persons mentally take on the new role before actually entering the position. Such new roles are more likely to be assumed if the anticipatory socialization experience is favorable, in the sense that the person believes the new position to be desirable.

My first argument is that the possible effect of leaders is limited by the fact that succession to leadership positions is itself highly constrained through processes of both organizational and individual selection. If leadership selection is constrained, the observed variation in behavior will also be constrained. This limits the opportunity to observe much leadership effect.

Constraints on leader behavior

Analyses of leadership have frequently presumed that leadership style or leader behavior was an independent variable that could be selected or influenced almost at will to conform to what research would find as the best leadership style. Certainly those organizational theorists who emphasized the importance of managerial style, such as Likert (1961) and McGregor (1966), implicitly assumed that once persons knew which leader behavior would increase effectiveness, such behavior could be implemented. Even the theorists who took a more contingent view of appropriate leadership behavior, with a few exceptions, assumed that with proper insight, appropriate leader behavior could be produced. Fiedler (1965), noting how hard it was to change leadership styles, suggested changing the conditions of the situation rather than the person; but this was an unusual suggestion in the context of the prevailing literature. Leadership style was something to be selected strategically by the manager, according to the variables of the particular leadership theory.

Such an approach neglects the fact that the leader himself is embedded in a social system. In the terms of Kahn, Wolfe, Quinn, and Snoek (1964), the leader also has a role set, in which members have expectations for appropriate behavior and in which persons holding various forms of power can attempt to influence the leader. Anyone who has ever held a leadership role recognizes that the possession of formally derived organizational authority does not leave the leader in complete, unilateral control over the situation. The leader himself has a superior, peers, and subordinates—all of whom have expectations for his behavior and all of whom have some means of enforcing these expectations. The discussion by Kahn et al. (1964) of role pressures indicates that behavior of persons in an organization is constrained by the demands of others in their role sets. Thus, decisions concerning the selection of appropriate behaviors are influenced by social processes. Pressures to conform to expectations of peers and subordinates and to the demands of superiors are all relevant in determining actual leadership behavior.

Leader behavior, however, is not only constrained by the social pressures derived from the social environment. Leaders also find that they have unilateral control over fewer resources and fewer policies than they might expect. Power is shared in organizations. Even at very high positions, the amount of discretion the leader has is limited. Investment decisions, larger than a relatively small amount, may require approval of others, including the board of directors. Hiring and promotion decisions may be accomplished by committees. Policies concerning organizational strategy may require consultation with others in the organization. Therefore, the amount of complete personal discretionary control over organizational actions is limited.

External factors

Many factors that may affect organizational performance remain outside the leader's control, even if he were to have complete discretion over major areas of organizational decisions. Consider, for example, the executive in a construction firm. Costs are largely determined by the operation of commodities and labor markets over which the executive has little, if any, control. Demand is largely affected by interest rates and the availability of mortgage money. These, in turn, are affected by governmental policies over which the executive has little influence.

This is certainly not the only case in which organizational performance is affected by external contingencies not controlled by the organization. School superintendents have little influence on birth rates and community economic development, both of which profoundly affect school system budgets. The administrator may react more or less successfully to the contingencies as they arise, and he may have better or worse forecasting capability, but in terms of accounting for variations in organizational outcomes it is possible the leader accounts for relatively little compared with those external forces.

Second, the leader's success or failure may be, in part, due to circumstances unique to the organization, but still outside his control. Leaders attain positions in organizations that vary in terms of the strength and position of the organization. The choice of a new executive at Lockheed, IBM, or General Motors does not fundamentally alter a position of market and financial strength or weakness that has developed over years, which affects the leader's ability to make strategic changes, or the likelihood that the organization will perform well or poorly. Organizations have capacities—strengths and weaknesses—that are relatively enduring. The choice of a particular leader for a particular position has limited impact on these capabilities; hence, the leader would be expected to have relatively little effect on organizational performance.

Empirical evidence

Two studies have attempted to assess the effects of changes in leadership among major positions within organizations. In an examination of 167 business firms in thirteen industries over a twenty-year period, Lieberson and O'Connor (1972) attempted to allocate variance in sales, profits, and profit margins to one of four sources: year (general economic conditions), industry, company effects, and the effects of changes in the top executive position (either president or chairman of the board). These authors concluded that, compared with the other factors, administration had a limited effect on organizational outcomes, having the greatest effect on profit margins and the smallest effect on sales. In further analyses Lieberson and O'Connor attempted to examine the characteristics of the industries in which administration had relatively larger or smaller effects. In those instances in which the firms were highly capital intensive and in which sales were closely tied to the economic cycle, the effects of the chief executive on organizational performance were lower.

Using a similar analytical procedure, Salancik and Pfeffer (1977) examined the effects of mayors on city budgets for a sample of thirty U.S. cities. Data were collected on expenditures by budget category and tax receipts by major categories for the period 1951–1968. Variance in the amount and proportion of expenditures was apportioned to the year, the city, or the mayor. Again, the mayor effect was relatively small, with the city effect accounting for most of the variance. However, the data indicated that the mayor effect was larger for those expenditure categories that were not as directly tied to important interest groups. While mayors had small effects on police, fire, and highway budgets, relatively more effect was observed on expenditures for items such as libraries, parks, and hospitals. Salancik and Pfeffer argued that the effects of the mayor were limited by the relative absence of power to control many of the expenditures and tax sources as well as by the fact that the mayor's policies were constructed in response to demands from interest groups.

Pfeffer and Salancik (1975) examined the extent to which the behaviors selected by first-line supervisors were constrained by the expectations of others in their role set. These authors reported that variance in both task and social behaviors could be accounted for by role-set expectations, with task behaviors being more highly related to the expectations of the supervisor, and social behaviors being more highly related to the expectations of the subordinates. Further, Pfeffer and Salancik noted that the extent to which the supervisor attended to the demands of his boss or subordinates was a function of the similarity between the supervisor and the boss, the demands to produce made by the boss, and the relative power of the boss and the subordinates. This study provides support for my contention that leadership effects are limited because leadership behaviors are themselves constrained, and further develops some hypotheses concerning which of the conflicting expectations the supervisor will heed.

Selznick (1957) has argued that leadership does matter—particularly strategic leadership exercised at a critical point in the organization's existence. There is, obviously, not enough evidence to indicate either the effects of leadership or, more significantly, the conditions under which leadership might be expected to have more or less impact on organizational outcomes.

I should also note that the effect of leadership may vary depending upon what level in the organizational hierarchy is being discussed. Lieberson and O'Connor and Salancik and Pfeffer studied leadership effects of top organizational personnel, as did Selznick. But, for the most part, empirical studies of leadership as found in the organizational psychology literature have dealt with first-line supervisors or foremen, or people with relatively low organizational status (Hall, 1972). If leadership has an impact on organizations, it should certainly be more evident at higher organizational levels, where there is more discretion in decisions and activities. The need to examine leadership effects at varying hierarchical levels is obvious.

The process of selecting leaders

The belief in the importance of leadership is frequently accompanied by the belief that persons occupying leadership positions are selected and trained according to how well they can enhance the organization's performance. If leadership matters in affecting organizational outcomes, then this surely justifies efforts to enhance selection and training procedures. Belief in a leadership effect, in other words, leads to the development of a set of activities, including theory building, selection, and training oriented toward enhancing leadership effectiveness. The assumption underlying these activities is that they will enable those so selected or trained to assume leadership positions and lead their organizations to increased levels of performance.

I have already discussed the issue of leadership effect, but I should also consider the issue of how, in fact, leaders are selected in organizations. The impact of leadership is directly related to beliefs that leaders are selected on the basis of their capability to enhance organizational performance. In general, there are two classes of criteria that may govern the selection of persons to leadership positions. One set of criteria consists of those measures that are universally applied to all persons and are independent of the social relationship between the persons being selected and those doing the selecting. These universalistic criteria need not be valid or reasonable in order to be considered universalistic— the only requirement is that the criteria and their application are independent of social relationships among the actors. As Blau (1964) has noted, if all members of a society believe that age is to be considered favorably, then age is a universalistic standard of assessment. When, however, one's belief about the value of age is dependent on one's own age, then age is an example of particularistic criteria. Contrasted with universalistic criteria, therefore, are particularistic criteria, such as social similarity or familiarity. Nepotism, for instance, is an example of a particularistic criterion.

The question of whether persons are selected on the basis of universalistic or particularistic standards is important. The theory of bureaucracy and the concept of administrative rationality require that persons be evaluated universalistically, on the basis of contributions and performance in the organization (e.g., Udy, 1962). Turner (1960) has written of sponsored and contest mobility, connoting the difference between mobility based on social connections (sponsorship) and mobility based on some standards of merit (contest). Perrow (1972, p. 11), reviewing bureaucratic theory, also commented on the difficulty of using impartial assessment standards for hiring and promotion. He noted that since competence was hard to judge, very frequently familiarity was used as the criterion.

Beliefs about the bases for mobility and the allocation of organizational positions and rewards are important for social stability. As long as persons believe that positions are allocated based on universalistic standards, particularly when such standards presumably assess ability or merit, the individuals are more likely to be satisfied with the social order and their position in it. This satisfaction derives from the fact that the persons will believe they are where they are because of reasonable and fair criteria. Second, they will believe that the opportunity exists for mobility in the organization or the society if they enhance and improve their skills and performance.

Research on the bases for hiring and promoting has been concentrated in the examination of academic positions (e.g., Cole & Cole, 1973; Hargens, 1969; Hargens & Hagstrom, 1967). This is possibly the result of the availability of relatively precise and unambiguous measures of performance, e.g., the number of publications or the number of times a person's publications are cited. Evidence on the criteria used in selecting and advancing personnel in industry is more indirect.

First, there are a few studies, using both personality and other background information, that have attempted to predict either compensation or the attainment of a general management position of MBA students. In a study of 136 graduates of the Graduate School of Industrial Administration at Carnegie-Mellon University, Weinstein and Srinivasan (1974) found there was a correlation of .24 ($p < .05$) between graduate grade-point average and compensation for persons in staff positions, and .49 ($p < .01$) between compensation and grade-point average for persons in line positions. In multiple regression with other variables, only in the case of line managers did the grade-point average remain significant. These authors reported some evidence for a positive relationship between a mathematics and statistics major and salary, and for a positive effect of an engineering major on staff position compensation. While the results, using ability and training variables, indicate the ability to predict future success as assessed by compensation, the amount of variance explained is relatively low. For staff positions, less than 15 percent of the variance in 1969 compensation, adjusted for years of work experience, could be explained. While more variance could be explained in line manager compensation salaries, this may be because there was more variance.[1] Harrell has conducted an extensive series of follow-up studies of Stanford MBAs. He reported a correlation of .28 ($p < .01$) between grades and present compensation, and a negative

1. Duncan (1975, p. 65) argued that too much attention was focused on the R^2 value, noting that R^2 depends both on the causal model and on the population to which the model applies.

correlation ($r = -.20$, $p < .01$) between the verbal scores on the
Admission Test for Graduate Study in Business and compensation
(Harrell & Harrell, 1974). Again, the variance explained is relatively small. Adding various personality measures has typically
not brought the amount of variance explained above 20 percent
(e.g., Harrell, 1972; Harrell & Harrell, 1974). While there is evidence that managerial success can be predicted by background
factors, including intelligence and performance in school, there is
evidently a great deal of variance not accounted for by these
factors.

The second line of research bearing on this issue has investigated the characteristics and background of persons attaining
leadership positions within major organizations in the society,
with a related body of inquiry that has investigated the process of
tracking in educational institutions and the relationship between
university attendance and subsequent economic success. Mills
(1963) examined the business elite born between the years 1850
and 1879, and reported that the percentage with upper-class
origins was 41.3 percent (pp. 110–139). Warner and Abbeglen
(1955, p. 156) studied the corporate elite and reported that a
"check on the *Social Register* shows that less than half were
members, indicating that it takes time for those who come from
the lower ranks to achieve social recognition for their economic
and occupational accomplishments." In a study of 884 directors of
major corporations, Domhoff (1967) reported that 53 percent
were identifiably associated with the upper class. Other examina-
tions of the composition of boards and executive ranks of a variety
of institutions, including universities, business firms, and government bureaucracies, indicate a strong preponderance of persons
with upper-class backgrounds. The implication is that studies of
MBAs and other college graduates would account for more of
the variance in later career success if the father's occupation and
income were included in the analyses.

Finally, Granovetter (1974) empirically examined the process
of getting a job. The importance of personal contacts, or proper
positioning in the social network, for success in this process is
clearly demonstrated. Such contacts are developed partially
through attendance at the right universities. Even after controlling for the quality of student input, as measured by standard-

ized achievement tests, research has indicated that there are significant relationships between the rank (prestige) of the college and earnings (Reed & Miller, 1970; Wolfle, 1971) and with occupational attainment (Collins, 1971; Spaeth & Greeley, 1970). Karabel and Astin (1975) reported data indicating a relationship between social origin and the rank of the college attended, when ability is controlled. Thus, the dynamic model developed is one in which access to elite universities is affected by social status, and, in turn, social status and attendance at elite universities affect later career outcomes.

Clearly, evidence shows that succession to leadership positions is not strictly based on merit. Further, it might be argued that the filtering encountered in moving through organizational hierarchies operates to co-opt those with lower social origins but with outstanding ability, and to filter out persons with unconventional beliefs or modes of behavior (Domhoff, 1967). While it is not the purpose of this essay to argue unequivocally for the relevance of the concept of social class for understanding American society, it is important to note that, in a variety of contexts, authors have found (1) that universalistic criteria account for relatively small proportions of the variation in career achievement, and (2) social connections are important in obtaining a job, and there are correlations between social origins and subsequent career outcomes when ability is taken into account.

The implications of these findings for research on leadership are direct. If succession to leadership positions is determined more by social origins or social connections, then efforts to enhance managerial effectiveness with the expectation that this will lead to career success divert attention from the processes of stratification that are really operating in organizations. I have first suggested that leadership may not account for much variance in organizational outcomes. Now I am suggesting that merit or ability may not account for hiring and advancement. The two ideas are interrelated. If competence is hard to judge, or if, in fact, leadership competence may not affect organizational outcomes greatly, then familiarity, or social connections, may be used, and may be all that are required. The search for effective leadership styles may not predict the career success of persons with those styles when social connections and social origin are controlled. If neither organizational performance nor career success are related to leadership behaviors, then one must begin to question why leadership is of such profound interest.

Leadership as attributed influence

People continually seek to attribute the causes of various events to possible causal variables. If A gets promoted and B does not, observers attempt to understand why. Kelley (1971, p. 2) has conceptualized the layman as "an applied scientist, that is, as a person concerned about applying his knowledge of causal relationships in order to *exercise control* of his world." Kelley reviewed a series of studies dealing with the attributional process in which persons sometimes attributed causes correctly and reasonably, and other times they did not. Kelley concluded that persons were not only interested in understanding their world but in controlling it as well. "The view here proposed is that attribution processes are to be understood not only as a means of providing the individual with a veridical view of his world, but as a means of encouraging and maintaining his effective exercise of control in that world" (1971, p. 22). He noted a tension in attributional processes between the feasible and the important. He argued the controllable factors will have high salience as candidates for causal explanation, while a bias toward the more important causes may shift the attributional emphasis toward causes that are not controllable (1971, p. 23).

If Kelley is correct, then the emphasis on leadership derives partially from a desire to believe in the effectiveness and importance of individual action, which is more controllable than the contextual variables that may also affect results. Lieberson and O'Connor (1972) have made essentially the same point in introducing their study on the effects of top management changes on organizational performance. Given the desire for control and a feeling of personal power and effectiveness, organizational outcomes are more likely to be attributed to individual actions, regardless of their causes.

Persons tend to attribute an effect to one of its causes when the two covary over time (Kelley, 1971). Schopler and Layton (1972) have posited that the attributed power of an actor A is a function of the conditional probability of an actor B's doing something at time 2 as a result of A's intervention at time 1, rather than the likelihood that B would have done the same thing regardless of A's intervention. Attribution, consequently, involves the computation of subjective probabilities concerning the magnitude of effects and what might have happened if certain interventions had not been made. Such subjective probability estimates can easily be affected by the desire to find causality in the actions taken by individuals.

Leadership, like other forms of social influence, is attributed by observers. Social action, in other words, has meaning only through some phenomenological process. The identification of certain organizational roles as leadership positions tends to guide the construction of meaning in the direction of attributing effects to the actions of those positions. Bavelas (1960) has noted that leadership as a social influence process is really shared throughout a group. The functions of leadership—be they task accomplishment, group maintenance, or something else—are also likely to be shared throughout a group. But the fact that the functions associated with the concepts of leadership, influence, and power are shared throughout a group provides no simple and potentially controllable focus for attributing causality. Rather, the identification of one or a few leadership positions provides the observer with a simpler and more readily changeable model of reality. When causality is lodged in one or a few persons, rather than being a function of a complex set of interactions among all group members, changes are made by replacing or influencing the occupant of the leadership position, and the causes of organizational actions are easily identified with this simple structure. Gamson and Scotch (1964) noted that in baseball the firing of the manager served a scapegoating effect. One cannot fire the whole team. Occupants of a leadership position come to assume symbolic value, and the attribution of causality to those positions serves to reinforce the organizational construction of meaning that provides the appearance of simplicity and controllability.

Even if, empirically, leadership has little effect, and even if succession to leadership positions is not predicated on ability or performance, the belief in leadership effect and the belief in meritocratic succession serve a variety of functions in maintaining the social order. These beliefs provide a simple causal framework and a justification for the structure of the social collectivity. Further, and most important, they interpret social action in terms that indicate the potential for effective individual intervention or control. The personification of social causality serves too many uses to be easily overcome.

The leader is, in part, an actor. Through his statements and actions, the leader attempts to reinforce the operation of the attribution process that tends to attribute causality to that position in the social structure. Successful leaders, as perceived by the members of the social system, are those who can separate themselves from organizational failures and associate themselves with organizational successes. Since the meaning of action is socially constructed, this involves the manipulation of symbols to reinforce the desired process of attribution. For instance, if a manager knows that business in his division is about to improve because of the economic cycle, he may, nevertheless, engage in writing a lot of recommendations and undertake actions and changes that are highly visible and that will tend to identify him and his behavior closely with the division. If, on the other hand, the manager perceives failure or a decrement in performance coming, he will attempt to associate the division and its policies and decisions with others, particularly persons in higher organizational positions. At the same time, he will attempt to disassociate himself from the division's performance, occasionally even going so far as to transfer or move to another organization.

Conclusions

The theme of this study has been that the analysis of leadership and leadership process must be contingent on the intent of the researcher. If one is interested in understanding the causality of social phenomena as reliably and accurately as possible, then the concept of leadership is probably a poor place to begin. It seems that the effects of leadership are very much open to question, and there are various reasons to expect relatively little leadership effect. The examination of the situational variables that tend to accompany more or less leadership effect is, nevertheless, a worthwhile task. If, however, one is interested in understanding how observers construct social meaning, the concept of leadership and its associated mythology, such as the belief in meritocratic advancement, is important. Leadership is the outcome of an attribution process in which observers—in order to achieve a feeling of control over their environment—tend to attribute outcomes to persons rather than to context, and the identification of individuals with leadership positions facilitates this attribution process. The belief in meritocratic advancement helps to legitimate the position of the leader with respect to others in the group, as well as to provide the appearance of potential mobility.

This more phenomenological analysis of leadership directs attention to the process by which social causality is attributed. Further, attention is focused on the distinction between causality as perceived by group members and causality as assessed by an outside observer. Leadership is associated with a set of myths serving to reinforce a social construction of meaning that legitimates leadership role occupants, provides the belief in potential mobility for those not in leadership roles, and attributes social causality to leadership roles, thereby providing a belief in the effectiveness of individual control. In analyzing leadership I have suggested that its mythology and the process by which such mythology is created and supported should be separated from the analysis of leadership as a social influence process, constrained by role demands and operating within structural constraints as well.

References

Bavelas, A. Leadership: Man and function. *Administrative Science Quarterly*, 1960, 4, 491–498.

Berscheid, E., & Walster, E. *Interpersonal attraction.* Reading, Mass.: Addison-Wesley, 1969.

Blau, P. M. *Exchange and power in social life.* New York: Wiley, 1964.

Bowers, D. C., & Seashore, J. E. Predicting organizational effectiveness with a four-factor theory of leadership. *Administrative Science Quarterly*, 1966, 11, 238–263.

Cartwright, D. C., & Zander, A. *Group dynamics: Research and theory.* Evanston, Ill.: Row, Peterson, 1960.

Cole, J. R., & Cole, S. *Social stratification in science.* Chicago: University of Chicago Press, 1973.

Collins, B. E., & Guetzkow, H. A *social psychology of group processes for decision-making*. New York: Wiley, 1964.

Collins, R. Functional and conflict theories of stratification. *American Sociological Review*, 1971, **36**, 1002–1019.

Day, R. C., & Hamblin, R. L. Some effects of close and punitive styles of supervision. *American Journal of Sociology*, 1964, **69**, 490–510.

Domhoff, G. W. *Who rules America?* Englewood Cliffs, N.J.: Prentice-Hall, 1967.

Duncan, O. D. *Introduction to structural equation models*. New York: Academic Press, 1975.

Fiedler, F. E. Engineering the job to fit the manager. *Harvard Business Review*, 1965, **43**, 115–122.

Fiedler, F. E. *A theory of leadership effectiveness*. New York: McGraw-Hill, 1967.

Gamson, W. A., & Scotch, N. A. Scapegoating in baseball. *American Journal of Sociology*, 1964, **70**, 69–72.

Granovetter, M. *Getting a job*. Cambridge, Mass.: Harvard University Press, 1974.

Hall, R. M. *Organizations: Structure and process*. Englewood Cliffs, N.J.: Prentice-Hall, 1972.

Halpin, A. W., & Winer, J. A factorial study of the Leader Behavior Description Questionnaire. In R. M. Stogdill & A. E. Coons (Eds.), *Leader behavior: Its description and measurement*. Columbus: Ohio State University, Bureau of Business Research, 1957.

Hargens, L. L. Patterns of mobility of new Ph.D.'s among American academic institutions. *Sociology of Education*, 1969, **42**, 18–37.

Hargens, L. L., & Hagstrom, W. O. Sponsored and contest mobility of American academic scientists. *Sociology of Education*, 1967, **40**, 24–38.

Harrell, T. W. High earning MBA's. *Personnel Psychology*, 1972, **25**, 523–530.

Harrell, T. W., & Harrell, M. S. *Predictors of management success* (Technical Report No. 3). Stanford, Calif.: Stanford University, School of Business, 1974.

Heller, F., & Yukl, G. Participation, managerial decision-making, and situational variables. *Organizational Behavior and Human Performance*, 1969, **4**, 227–241.

Hemphill, J. K., & Coons, A. E. Development of the Leader Behavior Description Questionnaire. In R. M. Stogdill & A. E. Coons (Eds.), *Leader behavior: Its description and measurement*. Columbus: Ohio State University, Bureau of Business Research, 1957.

Hickson, D. J., Hinings, C. R., Lee, C. A., Schneck, R. E., & Pennings, J. M. A strategic contingencies' theory of intraorganizational power. *Administrative Science Quarterly*, 1971, **19**, 216–229.

Hollander, E. P., & Julian, J. W. Contemporary trends in the analysis of leadership processes. *Psychological Bulletin*, 1969, **71**, 387–397.

House, R. J. A path goal theory of leader effectiveness. *Administrative Science Quarterly*, 1971, **16**, 321–338.

Kahn, R. L., Wolfe, D. M., Quinn, R. P., & Snoek, J. D. *Organizational stress: Studies in role conflict and ambiguity*. New York: Wiley, 1964.

Karabel, J., & Astin, A. W. Social class, academic ability, and college "quality." *Social Forces*, 1975, **53**, 381–398.

Kelley, H. H. *Attribution in social interaction*. Morristown, N.J.: General Learning Press, 1971.

Kochan, T. A., Schmidt, S. S., & DeCotiis, T. A. Superior-subordinate relations: Leadership and headship. *Human Relations*, 1975, **28**, 279–294.

Korman, A. K. Consideration, initiating structure, and organizational criteria—a review. *Personnel Psychology*, 1966, **19**, 349–362.

Lieberson, S., & O'Connor, J. F. Leadership and organizational performance: A study of large corporations. *American Sociological Review*, 1972, **37**, 117–130.

Likert, R. *New patterns of management*. New York: McGraw-Hill, 1961.

Lippitt, R. An experimental study of the effect of democratic and authoritarian group atmospheres. *University of Iowa Studies in Child Welfare*, 1940, **16**, 43–195.

Lowin, A. Participative decision-making: A model, literature critique, and prescriptions for research. *Organizational Behavior and Human Performance*, 1968, **3**, 68–106.

McGregor, D. *Leadership and motivation*. Cambridge, Mass.: MIT Press, 1966.

Mills, C. W. *Power, politics, and people* (I. L. Horowitz, Ed.). New York: Oxford University Press, 1963.

Perrow, C. *Complex organizations: A critical essay*. Glenview, Ill.: Scott, Foresman, 1972.

Pfeffer, J., & Salancik, G. R. Determinants of supervisory behavior: A role set analysis. *Human Relations*, 1975, **28**, 139–154.

Reed, R. H., & Miller, H. P. Some determinants of the variation in earnings for college men. *Journal of Human Resources*, 1970, **5**, 117–190.

Salancik, G. R., & Pfeffer, J. Constraints on administrator discretion: The limited influence of mayors on city budgets. *Urban Affairs Quarterly*, 1977, **12**, 475–496.

Sales, S. M. Supervisory style and productivity: Review and theory. *Personnel Psychology*, 1966, **19**, 275–286.

Schopler, J., & Layton, B. D. *Attribution of interpersonal power and influence*. Morristown, N.J.: General Learning Press, 1972.

Schutz, A. *The phenomenology of the social world*. Evanston, Ill.: Northwestern University Press, 1967.

Selznick, P. *Leadership in administration*. Evanston, Ill.: Row, Peterson, 1957.

Spaeth, J. L., & Greeley, A. M. *Recent alumni and higher education.* New York: McGraw-Hill, 1970.

Thompson, J. D. *Organizations in action.* New York: McGraw-Hill, 1967.

Turner, R. H. Sponsored and contest mobility and the school system. *American Sociological Review,* 1960, **25,** 855–867.

Udy, S. H., Jr. Administrative rationality, social setting, and organizational development. *American Journal of Sociology,* 1962, **68,** 299–308.

Vroom, V. H. Some personality determinants of the effects of participation. *Journal of Abnormal and Social Psychology,* 1959, **59,** 322–327.

Vroom, V. H., & Yetton, P. W. *Leadership and decision-making.* Pittsburgh: University of Pittsburgh Press, 1973.

Warner, W. L., & Abbeglen, J. C. *Big business leaders in America.* New York: Harper, 1955.

Weick, K. E. *The social psychology of organizing.* Reading, Mass.: Addison-Wesley, 1969.

Weinstein, A. G., & Srinivasan, V. Predicting managerial success of master of business administration (MBA) graduates. *Journal of Applied Psychology,* 1974, **59,** 207–212.

Wolfle, D. *The uses of talent.* Princeton, N.J.: Princeton University Press, 1971.

Yukl, G. Toward a behavioral theory of leadership. *Organizational Behavior and Human Performance,* 1971, **6,** 414–440.

Zald, M. N. Who shall rule? A political analysis of succession in a large welfare organization. *Pacific Sociological Review,* 1965, **8,** 52–60.

Commentary

Defining and measuring leadership has proved to be a frustrating task. How to distinguish leadership from other processes of social influence is not clear; its dimensions are uncertain, and researchers' ability to analyze it statistically may have outstripped what is actually known about the phenomenon.

The evidence of the effects of leadership is also spotty, and the magnitude of these effects is unknown. After decades of chasing this mirage, it is time to ask: When is leadership important and when is it not? And most fundamentally: How much does it matter?

Pfeffer offers several reasons why the observed effects of leaders on organizational performance would be small.

First, the ambiguity of theoretical orientations and actual measurement of leadership probably mitigates the results.

Second, the selection process favors those that "fit." We tend to like and choose to associate with those we perceive as similar to ourselves. Studies suggest that factors such as social class and social connections are more important than merit in selecting leaders. Familiarity is easier to judge than competence, so those with familiar and acceptable social characteristics are selected and/or select themselves. If the selection process reduces possible variations in behavior or style, the observed variation in leadership behavior will also be limited. This, in turn, limits the chance of observing much leadership effect.

Third, leadership behavior has often been treated as an independent variable by researchers, as if increasing certain behaviors would increase the effectiveness of subordinates. Such an approach ignores the reality of organizations. Leaders are embedded in a social system where power is shared; they do not have unilateral control over the situation. Subordinates, peers, and superiors have expectations of leader behavior and means of enforcing these expectations.

Fourth, many critical organizational variables are outside the leader's control—cost and demand factors, general market position, natural disasters. Pfeffer cites evidence that leadership behaviors are constrained externally. Both social and environmental factors limit the effect of what leaders do.

The limited effect that leaders may have on organizational performance does not mean the field of study should be abandoned. Pfeffer suggests that much of leadership is attributional in nature. We prefer to attribute cause to individuals rather than to a complex set of interactions because vesting cause in individuals gives us a sense of control over our environment. One approach to leadership research is to examine how observers construct social meaning—how symbols, office, beliefs, and perceptions combine to form the myths of leadership. Another approach is to develop a general taxonomy of leadership—situations in which leadership is critical and situations in which it is not.

In the next chapter, Weick presents a conceptual framework for viewing the process of leadership. He, as does Pfeffer, questions the methods by which leaders have been studied and suggests ways of looking at what leaders do, rather than at the fossils of their spines.

MML

3. The Spines of Leaders

Karl Weick

There are three kinds of spines that suggest ways to redirect leadership research: steel spines, plastic spines, and bony spines. Using the imagery of spines, I want to develop the argument that the effective leader is a docile leader, and that we as researchers may have to become both unstatistical naturalists and differentiating generalists (Murray, 1967, p. 295) to learn more about leadership.

Steel Spines

The contour gauge

Here is a simple tool called a contour gauge or a pattern maker (see illustration on the following page). It is six inches long with 180 steel spines, and when this gauge is pressed against some firm object an imprint of the object is registered. This imprint allows the craftsman to duplicate the pattern of the object by tracing the imprint that is made on the gauge.

I think this gauge is a non-trivial prod to the imagination concerning issues of leadership. Consider a few characteristics of the gauge and its imprint. The imprint is not the original object itself; it is a composite event, a spurious object. The single parts of the representation are essentially independent of one another. There are *no* causal connections between the parts (spines) because each part is caused separately from the *outside*. Originally,

A portion of this work was supported by the National Science Foundation through Grant SOC75–09864.

Contour gauge

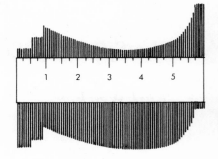

there was a unitary object that made the imprint, and the gauge now preserves a composite event.

Notice also that the gauge is value free and category free. It has no labels, and the imprint becomes meaningful only when you add values and categories to the display. For example, if you do not know what the original object was, and all you saw was the imprint, there would be no way for you to tell whether the original object was convex or concave. The imprint on the gauge is equivocal in its raw form; it resembles a pun. However, even though the imprint allows a duplexity of meanings, it is possible to operate on the imprint after it has been registered. By working on the imprint, I simply mean that you inspect it more closely, try out various possibilities as to what it might be, and punctuate the imprint into nouns and relations. For example, if you had an imprint of a table corner, then you could punctuate it into a line and a right angle.

Another property of this gauge is that it is a two-dimensional display that represents a three-dimensional object. This property will become crucial later on; but, for the moment, it is sufficient to note that the gauge is insensitive to variety. However, the gauge also preserves some variety. It preserves it in the sense that you can still project the image of the gauge and discover that some representations are "better" (i.e., more suggestive, more pragmatic) than other ones. If we put a light behind the gauge and then project its shadow onto a flat two-dimensional surface, we would find that when we rotated the gauge and changed the shape of the shadow, some of the images would be more suggestive than other ones.

But all of these properties are of secondary importance to three properties I want to emphasize.

Contour gauge as medium

Let us imagine that the gauge is a mediator between some core event and some final conclusion and action. This interpretation would be consistent with Heider's (1959) distinction between a thing and a medium in visual perception. There are three crucial variables that determine whether a medium is good or poor:

(1) the number of elements in the medium;
(2) the degree to which each element is independent of other elements;
(3) the degree to which the elements are externally, rather than internally, constrained.

Let me give some examples of differences between media. Consider whether sand or rock is a better medium to represent wind currents. It is usually easier to tell the pattern of prevailing winds in sand than in rock because there are more independent elements in sand that can represent the subtleties of wind speed and direction. Suppose we drape cloth or heavy paper over an object and ask a person to identify the object by feeling its contours. There is apt to be more accuracy when cloth is the medium, because again there are more independent elements subject to external constraint. Paper, on the other hand, is more internally constrained; consequently, it is a poorer medium to represent a thing. The use of expressive movements to judge personality also exhibits thing-medium properties. The general principle would be that the more significant expressive movements are, the less they are internally conditioned. "Therefore, facial expression is especially important because the anatomical structure is such that many different combinations of movement are possible" (Heider, 1959, p. 23).

With these three variables in hand, we can now begin to gather some strands and start thinking about leaders. So far, I have suggested that (1) objects can be represented by combining independent elements, (2) less internal conditioning means better mediation, and (3) the number of elements available for independent combination determines the sensitivity of the medium. Now all of this becomes consequential for leadership when we start to examine the image of the "leader as medium." The first thing we need to do to enliven this image is dispense with the implication that thing-medium relationships conclude at the eyeball. The examples I have used so far may seem to work mostly for visual and olfactory perception and, therefore, to be of limited help. I think it is more productive to think of a medium as any of the systems that register objects around us and not as some intervening space. Events seep into awareness and register through more avenues than our eyes and our noses, and the argument would be that a person becomes a better medium as he uses a greater number of channels and uses them independently of one another when he confronts the world. Thus, the crucial medium for a leader is not the space in front of him; instead it is the number of mechanisms to register events that he brings to a situation and the degree to which these mechanisms function simultaneously but independently.

There is warrant for treating a medium in this more extended sense. For example, Barker (1968) talks about the "medium of the receptor system" (p. 160), about the fact that "light and receptor systems must have the properties of media" (p. 161), and about people as media. Thus, we need to invoke the image of receptor systems and sense organs. In doing so, we can then entertain the possibility that the combining of independent receptor systems provides better mediation and more accurate perception of the core events implied by the composite. In turn, these richer interpretations by the leader should produce more adequate coping by his associates.

Errors in the contour gauge

A contour gauge can mislead. Imagine that we took this six-inch gauge and applied it to an object that was eight inches long. The imprint would be inaccurate. Imagine that these 180 spines were pressed against an object that undulated 360 times in the space of six inches. The imprint would be inaccurate. I have already mentioned that the gauge simplifies because it is two-dimensional and the object three-dimensional. Imagine what happens when some of the spines get bent, such that when one spine moves, it pulls others with it regardless of the shape of the object being sensed. By now these errors should be understandable items in terms of the three properties of a medium. This correspondence has a surprising outcome. In each of the examples I just gave, there is more variety in the object than there is in the medium. The object has eight inches, the gauge a mere six; the object changes direction 360 times, the gauge can change direction only 180 times; the object has three dimensions, the gauge a mere two. This suggests the appropriateness of adding a new notion, namely, the concept of requisite variety. This concept states that it takes variety to destroy, control, or regulate an object that can be contoured in 360 ways, and then we have to increase the variety of the contour gauge. If we fail to do so, the world of 360 contours will always be more complex than our systems to deal with it. Furthermore, when we are insensitive to complexity, we cannot predict or control what our outcomes will be when we deal with that environment. And the leader who cannot stabilize the outcomes and keep them constant will lose influence over his followers. The leader's variable behavior produces constant outcomes.

Let me mention three versions of requisite variety to be certain that the concept, which derives from engineering, is understood. "If, for instance, a press photographer should deal with 20 subjects that are (for exposure and distance) distinct, then his camera must obviously be capable of at least 20 distinct settings if all the negatives are to be brought to a uniform density and sharpness" (Ashby, 1969, p. 117). Buckley (1968) describes the principle this way: "The variety within a system must be at least as great as the environmental variety against which it is attempting to regulate itself" (p. 495). A more recent version of this same point is found in Gregory Bateson's 1968 conference on conscious purpose (M. C. Bateson, 1972, pp. 158–159). Several people at the conference were rather startled when Fred Attneave uttered in a matter-of-fact tone, "We simply have to face the fact that we have vulgar nervous systems." Nervous systems are "vulgar simply because they are finite; they would have to be infinite to represent the universe in its complete complexity. I think it is an exceedingly important fact of life that we have to simplify. It's a matter of trying to find the simplifications that are necessary to our ends." Bateson observed, however, that there seemed to be a way to beat the vulgarity game and Warren McCulloch concurred. The essence of Bateson's point was that "one of the things about the nervous system that gives it a potentiality to be less vulgar than one might have expected is the enormous hierarchic structure in the thing, in which you get representations in depth." By representations in depth, Bateson meant basically that when some premise is embodied in the brain it ramifies, it induces other relations with other things in the brain; complexity is added, and the complexity of the environment can then be represented more adequately.

One drawback to the concept of requisite variety is that it has been hard, in the case of human beings, to specify just what it means to increase variety. Bateson's quotation suggests that imposing structure on retained content enhances variety. Both Pribram (1967) and Bateson (1972) have argued that habituation and the development of defenses in depth allow one to process more of what is occurring. Pribram talks about an increase in requisite variety as expanding the repertoire of actions with which one can approach a situation. All of these proposals have a certain plausibility, but they still seem sterile.

What I would like to propose is that requisite variety be defined in terms of the properties of a good medium. This is essentially a content-free definition. The thrust of this proposal would be that you gain variety and a better probability of control by creating greater independence among elements, increasing the number of elements, and decreasing the density of internal constraints. I am arguing that improving mediation is equivalent to raising requisite variety. This is not as simple a proposal as it may sound. I shall save some of the intricacies for later, but let me show two of the complications.

The first complication turns on my description of requisite variety in a content-free way. Many people who talk about requisite variety argue that complicated human beings are better able to register the complications in the world around them. These complications within the individual are often described in terms of specific experiences. A person who was once a mental patient and now manages his neuroses well is seen as more complicated than a person who merely manages his neuroses well. The one-time mental patient has a greater variety of experience than does the stranger to the asylum. But this greater variety is defined in terms of specific experiences. Regardless of what confronts the complicated person, he has something personal to which he can refer these various happenings. As a consequence, he can sense and regulate more of what impinges on him. This is the view that requisite variety resides in the diversity of experiences retained by the person.

My suggestion that increments in requisite variety are produced by enrichment of medium qualities says nothing about content. Conceivably, a person who has the same experience over and over could have greater requisite variety than is true for the person who bounces among experiences. This is plausible if the one-dimensional man were able to register that single experience in a richer and richer fashion. If, over time, I have a greater number of independent elements that I direct at a thing, then that thing will register differently and in more detail. And that greater complication in the registering mechanisms is obviously available for sensing when new events are experienced. It is this sense in which medium enhancement may be a useful means to preserve adaptability while still adapting to a specific niche.

I would hazard the guess that requisite variety viewed in terms of specific experiences rather than in terms of medium properties may be impossible to untangle. The two interpretations may be hopelessly confounded. I say that because if more of an object, any object, can get into my mind regardless of its content (this would be due to medium enrichment), then the reservoir of actual experiences that I have will be fuller and more varied. This is an important confounding to clarify, if possible, because it has very different implications for how one would equip leaders to have the variety requisite to cope with their environments. It is a problem worth considering, but at this time I simply must indicate feeling more favorable toward the content-free view of requisite variety because it is more manageable conceptually, has a certain plausibility, makes adaptive sense, and fits a long-standing way of parsing the problem of perception (e.g., Zener & Graffron, 1962).

Let me show in a slightly different way some of the dilemmas of mediation and requisite variety. Heider (1958) discusses the problem of ambiguous mediation. By this, he means a state of equivocal information, a state in which the information conveyed implies more than one core event. In other words, knowing the output, one cannot say for certain what input generated that output. Different core events can be derived from the same display. A figure-ground reversal would be an example of ambiguous mediation.

Now the puzzles in the case of ambiguous mediation are substantial. First of all, ambiguous mediation could occur when there are vague core events. This would be the case if these events produced very few offshoots from which one could reconstruct the core. This scarcity of offshoots could suggest several unitary events. More likely, however, is the possibility that the problem is in the medium. But what we cannot tell is whether the problem is a content problem—the observer does not have a template, or image of idea, against which he can match the external input—or whether the problem is a medium problem. Namely, he senses the object poorly because the medium is impoverished. In either case, the observer has less variety in his processing system than exists in the object, but the problem is what he should do to increase this variety.

Despite these potential problems, the basic proposal is straightforward. First, the quality of leadership may be affected by the degree to which the leader retains sufficient variety to control the variety that confronts him. Second, the leader increases his requisite variety by operations that improve his medium qualities.

Living between two spurious events

So far the line of argument being developed is decidedly one-way. I have been talking about sequences that originate in some core event outside the person, are mediated by independent elements in a variety of media, and terminate in a composite that is a spurious thing. But once the object is reconstructed inside the person, what happens when the person takes action? Here is where the idea of the leader as medium gains a great deal of its power.

Originally I had thought that the idea of the leader as medium was attractive because it furnished a rather tidy way to think about a classic problem, namely, the issue of perception vs. action. At first blush, it seems that a person fully using his medium qualities destroys his potential for action. This seems plausible because when one acts against an environment, he should have the maximum amount of thing-like qualities in order to make some difference in that environment (e.g., proactive man). The actor wants to be internally constrained when he acts, externally constrained when he builds representations of the environment in which he wants to act. Since it will be tough to make full use of both of these mutually exclusive states, leaders will tend to be more skilled at either action or perception. That is moderately interesting, but hardly news.

What is more interesting is the distinct possibility that enhancing medium qualities facilitates *both* perception and action. Remember that earlier I talked about the face as a good medium to represent core events in the person being observed. A crude way to restate that example is to say that some core event *inside* the person is responsible for constraining some of the independent elements in the face. The central idea that makes plausible the assertion that the organism "lives between two spurious units of composite processes" is the idea that the "organs of the body which affect things directly must be as nearly as possible perfect *mediators* for the action impulses coming *from* the brain" (Heider, 1959, p. 32, italics added). Until now we have been concerned with the person as a mediator of external objects. That is the path going from outside to inside. Now we are adding the point that the person is also an action mediator. The core event in the case of action mediation is an action impulse. This impulse is mediated by organs, and the impulse terminates in a spurious activity directed toward the environment. The action impulse, due to the fact that action is mediated, will also be imperfect and a composite event. A person will never do exactly what he wanted to do. What he wanted to do is the action impulse that, through faulty mediation, will be represented externally in somewhat incomplete form. Again the degree of this incompleteness will depend on the quality of the medium.

To the extent that object mediation and action mediation are done by the same systems, then medium enrichment will improve the quality of both perception and action. Take the hand, for example. As an object mediator, the hand is more perfect the more the single fingers are independent of each other, the less rigid are the fingers, the smaller the two-point threshold, and the less internally constrained the fingers are by such things as cold or arthritis. Now these properties also enhance the hand as a mediator of action. Those same independent, nonrigid fingers can execute action impulses with greater control than is the case for organs that are poorer media.

The unusual imagery suggested here is that the person lives somewhere between two imperfect worlds. He never does quite what he wants with respect to quite what he thinks is out there. But his miscalculations and misperceptions should decline the more requisite variety he has relative to the complexity that confronts him from outside and inside his own skin.

Summary

Here are the ideas we will be using in the remaining discussions:

1. The crucial items in a contour gauge when viewed as a medium are the number of spines, the independence among the spines, and the extent to which the pattern of the spines is externally conditioned.
2. The contour gauge is a reasonable model of mediator processes as these occur in leaders.
3. A leader gains control over the variety that confronts him by increasing his medium qualities. To gain requisite variety, the leader raises the number of elements that are available for registering and increases independent functioning among the elements.
4. To the degree that a receptor system also mediates action impulses, medium enhancement raises both the accuracy of the representations and the suitability of the action.
5. The argument to be developed is that many conventional prescriptions for leaders transform the leaders into poor media. Furthermore, inferior mediation by the leader may be responsible for those occasions when presumably good leadership actually handicaps a group and makes it less adaptable.

6. If a person does not register information, he cannot control it, organize it, edit it, or rearrange it. I am concerned with what the leader has to work on, what his raw materials are, and when he conducts analyses of situations.

7. The followers basically use the leader as a contour gauge. The leader is their medium with respect to the environment. This means that the followers see through the eyes of their leader. He gets the pictures for them and reveals various projections of these impressions to them. In that sense the leader is an *n*-dimensional gauge, and he makes 3D or 2D or 1D slices of the display for the followers. Viewed in this way, the leader continually reveals novel aspects of the situation, and it is this novelty that gives him power. People rely on the leader's pictures because he gets more accurate and more diverse or more suggestive pictures than do any of the followers.

8. The leader does have to be active in the sense that he must expose himself to the environment in order to get imprints. He must be active if he is to register things. It is this sense in which he must be externally constrained rather than internally constrained. If a leader is going to be externally constrained, he has to put himself in the presence of objects that can constrain him.

9. Sooner or later the leader will want to issue commands. Then, but only then, he has to become more internally constrained. If he wants to control in the sense of keeping outcomes constant, he has to be tightly coupled with the environment and loosely coupled within himself. If he wants to command, then he has to become loosely coupled with the environment so that he is not controlled by it and tightly coupled within himself to take action.

Plastic Spines

The Protean lifestyle

There is an interesting sense in which the steel spines I have been talking about so far are in fact plastic spines, plastic in the sense of being docile, impressionable, changeable, and impermanent.

The plastic imagery is appropriate because it is precisely this imagery that *Time* magazine used when describing Marcello Mastroianni as a neocapitalist hero "with a spine made of plastic napkin rings" (Lifton, 1971, p. 301). What is even more interesting is that this comment about Mastroianni's spine is cited in an article arguing that an increasingly prominent contemporary lifestyle is the Protean lifestyle.

The name derives from Proteus in Greek mythology, a character who could change his shape with relative ease. What Proteus found difficult "and would not do unless seized and chained, was to commit himself to a single form, the form most his own, and carry out his function of prophecy" (Lifton, 1971, p. 299). Lifton describes the Protean man of contemporary society in this way:

> The Protean style of self-process, then, is characterized by an interminable series of experiments and explorations—some shallow, some profound—each of which may be readily abandoned in favor of still new psychological quests. The pattern in many ways resembles what Eric Erikson has called "identity diffusion" or "identity confusion," and the impaired psychological functioning which those terms suggest can be very much present.

Having set up that preamble, Lifton then gets to the controversial punch line. "But it is important to stress that the Protean style is by no means pathological as such, and, in fact, may well be one of the functional patterns of our day. . . . Just as elements of the self can be experimented with and readily altered, so can idea systems and ideologies be embraced, modified, let go of, and reembraced all with a new ease."

This characterization is all the more interesting because it was independently discovered by Zurcher (1972) when he compared answers to the Kuhn and McPartland Twenty Statements Test over the last several years. He found clear evidence that people have shifted from describing themselves in terms of institutionalized roles (e.g., professor, father, citizen) to describing themselves in terms of characteristic ways of acting (e.g., helpful, flexible). What is interesting is that Zurcher interprets this as a shift from seeing oneself in static terms to an emphasis on self as process, the very same emphasis that Lifton mentioned. And, as Lifton does, Zurcher sees this shift as functional. It is functional not to identify oneself with social structure when that social structure is undergoing changes. Zurcher refers to this phenomenon as "the mutable self," a phrase that is about as synonymous with Protean lifestyle as one could hope for. Lifton and Zurcher's enthusiasm for this commentary on human resilience is counterbalanced by those who feel that these two observers have missed the point. To argue that it is good to have centerless people when society has no center is to condone pathology rather than to do something about it. The opposite argument has been articulated by Michael Maccoby (1972, pp. 174–191).

My reason for mentioning these two lifestyles is that they provide good examples of just what a leader might look like if his medium qualities were fully developed. In each portrait fragments are common, there is no single identity, absurdity is commonplace, external determination is the rule, and, in John Cage's words, "nothing is off-limits in attending" for these people. It may be that as leaders become better mediums, they will resemble more closely the Protean or mutable lifestyle. And both of those lifestyles seem to be unlikely candidates for leadership as we routinely think of that activity. But if we want some idea of how a leader as medium might look, then the image of a person with plastic napkin rings as a spine is of more than passing interest.

Implications for thinking about leadership

Let me describe some of the implications of the possibility that the good leader is a good medium. Incidentally, there is more than a touch of irony in that phrase if one recalls that a medium can be a person who is susceptible to supernormal agencies such as is the case with spiritualists.

1. The good leader is docile. The good leader is docile in the sense that many of his constraints are external rather than internal. I think this is a crucial point. There seems to be a definite "macho mystique" in writing about leadership. Leaders are described as people who take charge, take initiative, initiate structure, and are decisive, firm, consistent, striking, charismatic, forceful, and strong. Every one of those tendencies implies that the person exhibiting them will be an inferior medium. Such a person would not be very perceptive. All of those characteristics are accomplished by reducing fragments, increasing internal constraints, and by increasing dependencies among elements. To be decisive means to act in a nonfragmented manner. Self-contradictions, ambivalence, inconsistencies, hesitance are the antithesis of decisiveness, though they may be the very epitome of mediation. The leader who exhibits some tendency (e.g., aggression) and its opposite (e.g., pacifism) is viewed as wishy-washy, confused, or hypocritical. What seems to be given less attention is the possibility that owning up to a tendency *and* its opposite doubles the elements that a person has available for potential influencing.

2. *Docile leaders provide more diverse images to their followers.*
If one adopts a retrospective view of action and argues that people know what they have done only after they do it, then an unstudied tendency that may differentiate among leaders is the extent to which they serve up interesting images to their followers regarding what they have been doing. Furthermore, the better leader may be a person who both serves up heroic images and frequently reinterprets past actions. The leader who rewrites history, who rewrites it in a bold and interesting manner, and who rewrites it frequently may create considerable compliance among his followers.

The relevance of this line of argument to the present discussion is that the more medium-like a leader is, the more images he should be able to invent and make available to his followers. And to the extent that those followers thrive on seeing themselves engaged in interesting activities housed in interesting worlds, this leader should be influential.

3. *It is a handicap to be a natural-born leader.* The point here is simple. If there is such a thing as a "natural-born leader," then that should be detrimental because it means that the person so described has never been a follower. His images and information are more impoverished and more simplified than are those of a person who has been both a leader and follower. The same line of argument can be used with respect to other so-called natural talents that in actuality may be natural blinders.

4. *Leaders who are good media will have shorter time horizons.* This suggestion derives from the work of Richard Goodman (1973). He has considered the relationship between how well an organization knows its environment and how far into the future it looks before taking conscious action. He argues that as knowledge gets richer, an organization's focus becomes more short term, and the time horizon shrinks. This shrinkage is predicted to occur because organizations tend to focus attention on areas where progress can be made, and rich knowledge tends to pinpoint immediate targets of opportunity. As richness of knowledge declines, the present is perceived as simpler and the time horizon lengthens.

The direct extension of this argument is the prediction that as a leader becomes more medium-like, he will have a shorter time horizon. His attention will focus more on the here and now. That is interesting because it is often remarked that groups are solution-oriented rather than problem-oriented. That has always been presumed to occur because groups have poor intelligence and cannot tolerate uncertainty. I know of no one who has argued that *rich* knowledge is responsible for solution centering. Yet that should be an outcome if rich knowledge promotes a shortened time horizon. Solution finding should have a shorter time horizon than problem identification.

Notice also that one could reinterpret the strategy of disjointed incrementalism (Hirschman & Lindblom, 1962) given the argument being developed here. Originally it was argued that organizations solve problems in an incremental, disjointed, gradual manner, inching from problem to problem because of the complexity and uncertainty in their inputs. The original argument was that this was a moderately rational response when the organization was overloaded and could not process the complex inputs. However, it is also possible to argue that if an organization has a rich knowledge of the environment, this will shorten its time horizon, and in turn will direct the corporation toward incremental rather than long-range plans and actions.

It would also be fascinating to learn whether richer knowledge has any effect on the speed with which time seems to pass. If the time horizon shortens, does time also seem to pass more swiftly? The answer to that is crucial because there is good evidence that when people overestimate the speed with which time is passing, they will consider a much shallower set of alternatives in decision making and will make poorer choices among these alternatives.

5. *The docile leader is a better controller.* Two common activities of leaders, command and control, are often confused. Command and control differ in at least one crucial way, and it is this difference that suggests why a leader with good medium qualities may be better able to control.

The crucial difference between command and control is that to control a thing, you have to listen to it. That is not the case with command. If you want to control something and issue some kind of message, you have to listen to see if the message is understood. "Suppose you're drilling troops; the first thing you do is you order what is to be done and you listen to that come back. You yell 'right by squads' and it comes back 'right by squads.' Only then do you say 'march'!" (M. C. Bateson, 1972, p. 205). If you want to control something, you have to have information about its current state and current activity.

This is not a novel point, but it does need to be stressed. Leadership in the sense of control is not a unilateral activity, but it is easy to overlook the fact that listening is crucial. It is seldom possible to dominate without being affected by what is dominated. The point is that sensitivity to this aspect of control is virtually built-in when the leader is a good medium. A good medium is by definition a sensitive listener-receiver, and the probability that such a person would issue vacuous commands should be lower.

6. *Leadership improvement may involve training in data splitting.* By now the distinction between thing and medium may seem rather bland, and I would like to return to the notion long enough to illustrate just exactly what a dramatic accomplishment a thing-medium attribution is. The nature of this accomplishment has been beautifully summarized by Karl Duncker (quoted in Heider, 1958, p. 66):

the sense organ exhibits the . . . astonishing ability to split in varying ways, according to circumstances, one and the same datum of stimulation; for example, one given retinal intensity of light, one kind of light, one retinal size, one retinal form, one position, the completeness and clearance of stimulation, etc., into the two phenomenal components: property of the thing (e.g., object color, object size, object form, object position, completeness and clearness of the object) and property of the intervening circumstances (e.g., illumination, distance, orientation, and position with regard to the eye, covering or veiling medium). This makes it possible to attribute a large class of changes not to the things themselves, but to the respective intervening factors.

If you listen to a radio program that is muddled by static, there is a single impression, yet you are able to separate it into two components. If you wear glasses and view a scene without your glasses, you can split that single perception into its thing and medium components. The blur in vision is not regarded as a property of the object. If you view a scene through sunglasses, you can typically separate thing from medium components. What is remarkable is that errors are so infrequent given the complexity of the splitting.

The relevance of this splitting for leadership enhancement is the possibility that you could train people to do better separations between mediational and object properties. Typically, this splitting is seen as dependent on age and, therefore, not particularly malleable. Yet it seems that much of the recent writing by people like Gardner Murphy (1975), Annie Dillard (1975), Carlos Castaneda (1972), and Lewis Thomas (1974) could be read as arguing for experiences that produce better differentiation of mediational from object properties. Obviously, there are some radical assumptions about transfer of training built into this argument. Essentially, it is being argued that, somehow, greater sophistication at splitting single data into thing and medium components enhances the general level of requisite variety.

7. Self-acceptance improves medium qualities. The point to be made here is straightforward, yet I call it to your attention simply because it is another example of an intervention in an apparently unrelated area that might affect the quality and kind of leadership that is exhibited.

The basic point is that denial of personal characteristics creates dependence among elements, thereby producing poorer mediation. When people deny and distort some of their tendencies, this works against medium qualities in two ways. First, denial leads to a more simplistic view of self, which means that there is a reduction in the complexity of external objects that can be apprehended. Second, denial takes vigilance and close monitoring to sustain it, lest the denials be contradicted by reality. This hypervigilance not only occupies all channels normally available for perception, but it also increases dependencies among the elements, thereby reducing mediation.

Fenichel's (1945) description of symptoms in neurosis is unusually appropriate to illustrate how a lack of self-acceptance degrades the quality of the medium. Fenichel notes that a common complaint of neurotics is disturbances in the ability to concentrate. He goes on to observe that

> The first reason such patients cannot concentrate on a conscious task lies in their unconscious preoccupation with a more important internal task, their defensive struggle. In severe cases, archaic and integrated activities replace the more recently acquired and differentiated ones; a resistance is developed against differentiated tasks and even against the acceptance of new stimuli, the reaction to which would need new amounts of energy. [1945, p. 185]

Notice the words and phrases like "preoccupation," "differentiated activities disappear," "new stimuli are deflected," "differentiated tasks are avoided," and "people regress toward the integrated." In each case there is an erosion of the medium, a simplification of the organism, a movement away from requisite variety.

If leaders could see themselves in the intricacy that they have, especially when components of that intricacy suggest ambivalent tendencies, then those leaders should be better able to appreciate equally complicated systems, people, or events. Consider, for example, a source of complication for women mentioned by M. C. Bateson (1972, p. 287). What would it "mean for human adaptation if you blotted out the emotional irregularities that go with the female menstrual cycle, changing the experience women have of their bodies; one of the things that you would be blotting out is a diversity that may be the basis of responding to some other kind of diversity." Thus, these irregularities may induce more sensitivity to external complexity than if they were denied or ignored or never noticed.

But the general point is that deficiencies in self-acceptance have obvious costs in psychological pain. For our discussion, these deficiencies also have other less obvious costs because they erode the variety a leader has available to control and regulate the variety that confronts him. People can vulgarize their own nervous systems by lapses in self-acceptance. Self-acceptance, by definition, means acceptance of fragments. And acceptance rather than denial will potentially make these fragments available as independent media.

8. *Poetry enhances medium qualities.* I realize that my suggestions about characteristics that differentiate better leaders from poorer ones are becoming more and more speculative, but the inclusion of poetry is anchored in a concrete nuance of requisite variety.

Earlier I noted that one of the problems with requisite variety is that human beings find it difficult to gain access to the complexity that is in them. Essentially, this entire essay involves variations on the theme of how to enhance requisite variety. The "reason why poetry is important for finding out about the world is because in poetry a set of relationships gets mapped onto a level of diversity in us that we don't ordinarily have access to. So we need poetry as knowledge about the world and about ourselves, because of this mapping from complexity to complexity" (M. C. Bateson, 1972, p. 289).

If poetry activates latent channels or elements through which both action and objects can be mediated, if poetry decouples the ties among elements such that each registers independently of the other, then it is not idle or irresponsible to propose that there is a bit of the poet in every leader or vice versa. The poetry is crucial, not only because it proliferates the images leaders have available, but also because it complicates the structure with which the leader meets a complicated world.

9. *Medium management is a leadership tactic.* Until now I have talked about thing-medium relationships in a rather sanguine manner. If a leader knows what promotes perception, namely the three variables that I have mentioned repeatedly, then that same leader could prevent perception by eliminating a good medium. So far, I have basically assumed, the clearer the better; the more elements the better, etc. I have been noticeably silent (and perhaps anachronistic) by *not* invoking contingency jargon, by not inserting "it all depends" before every hint of an assertion. Avoidance of that pose has been intentional because I want to lay out a fairly compact argument that is then available for amendment, replacement, or indifference.

The point to be made here is that medium management, intentionally expanding or reducing the number of elements, can also be seen as a powerful means of control available to the leader. The attractiveness of this proposal is that it focuses our attention on a restricted set of variables and raises the probability that we will notice something that is interesting.

What is even more interesting is that even when we expand the discussion to include media management as tactic, previous ideas still retain their force. If we argue that medium management improves, the more sensitive the leader is to thing-medium splitting, then we come full circle to the proposition that medium management is a direct function of the richness of the leader as medium. That is not surprising when you consider that a person who is skilled at partialling variance into that which is attributable to object and that which is attributable to medium should be in an ideal position to know what to manipulate if he wants to promote or prevent perception.

10. *Viewing the leader as medium intersects crucial issues in organizational theory.* The idea of a medium is useful for pulling together different themes in the organizational theory literature. If these strands and those concerning leadership can be combined with a common set of labels, then our chances of improving the quality of leadership research should improve.

I think there are numerous points of entry where things of interest to organizational theorists can intrude. For example, if we talk about stable interstructured behaviors, recurring mutual equivalence structures, repetitive double interacts, reverberating cycles, or stable subassemblies, in each case the events being referred to are patterned, repetitive, stable over time, and therefore internally constrained. And being internally constrained, these are the "things" of interest to organizational theorists. And they are the things that will be registered more or less accurately by leaders of those groups, depending on their medium qualities.

Consider another problem that seems potentially remote from leadership, yet which is joined with it by means of the shared concepts of medium and requisite variety. There has long been an interest in trying to explain why a stranger who visits a foreign group sees that group more objectively and in greater detail than does the native. Simmel (1950), for example, has written in detail and with sensitivity on the issue of "the objectivity of the stranger." However, no one has yet viewed this presumed objectivity in terms of thing-medium issues; yet this set of ideas fits the problem rather economically.

It is common to find that strangers, when they visit a foreign group, are disoriented, a form of disorientation called culture shock. One way to think about disorientation is to see the elements that normally constitute an identifiable individual as becoming independent, very well proliferating in number. These momentary disruptions render the person more susceptible to external constraint; consequently he registers more of what is happening around him, even if he cannot find the nouns and verbs to label and manage these happenings. This has some interesting implications. Disorientation under these conditions could become a vicious circle. More registry leads to more fragmentation leads to more registry until the person, through one means or another, must ruthlessly close down his channels and/or arrest the fragmentation (enter the "thrill" of finding another American amid foreign chaos).

Gaining some popularity among organizational theorists is the view that organizations are garbage cans, organized anarchies, loosely coupled assemblages, entities that keep falling apart, or units that make themselves up as they go along. What all of these images share is a presumption that ties among components said to constitute the organization are much weaker, indeterminant, and overlapping on fewer common elements; that they are more subject to coincidence, accident, and time flows than has been previously recognized. What has not yet been pursued is the possibility that such loosely joined structures or empty worlds are good media. If this possibility is even plausible, then it argues that organizational chaos is sensible. It further argues that if one could measure organizations on the degree to which they have medium qualities, the greater the medium qualities, the better their competitive position. Measuring an organization that is a good *medium* should be difficult because this quality should itself be imperceptible. The nuances of that possibility, or where its pursuit might take us, are momentarily beyond my time and talents. But I think the question is worth pursuing; it may well hold some unexpected answers concerning why our conventional pronouncements about leadership can go awry when they are implemented in loosely coupled worlds.

As a final comment on loose coupling, and the way in which medium concepts reshuffle our thinking, consider how loose coupling has been invoked by at least one writer who has used the idea. Glassman (1973) has argued that when units are loosely coupled to their environments (e.g., legislators are buffered from the whims of their constituents by four-year terms of office), this is beneficial because it allows the unit to persist, and it serves as a buffer against capricious changes in the unit's environment. Essentially, the environment is prevented from registering by virtue of loose coupling.

However, the argument that I have developed suggests a rather different picture. If loose coupling can be viewed in this way, then loose coupling should allow the environment to register more fully and richly rather than not at all. Thus, if we observe that a loosely coupled system adapts quite well and if we try to explain this adaptation, we can say either that it survives because it is protected from environmental buffeting, or that it survives because it richly registers the nature of that environment. Those are rather different explanations. One says that closedness promotes survival; the other that openness promotes survival. What is even more intriguing is that both of these modes, relabeled preparation and participation, are viewed as ways to achieve requisite variety within Pribram's (1967) theory of the neurological bases of emotion.

Bony Spines

Let me conclude these remarks by introducing my final set of spines, those made of bone. There is a certain irony in this conference because one way to phrase our task is to say that we are trying to figure out how to lead leadership research. If we knew how to productively lead researchers into this topic, there would be no need for them to attempt its study.

But it is clear to me there are some less productive ways to approach the topic of leadership. Let me express my gratitude to John Steinbeck, both for alerting me to these lapses, and especially for describing these lapses in spiny imagery. During one of Steinbeck's expeditions through the Gulf of California (the Sea of Cortez), he became fascinated with a species of fish called the Mexican sierra. The Mexican sierra is shaped like a trout, has brilliant blue spots, ranges from fifteen inches to two feet, is slender, is a very rapid swimmer, is classified with mackerel-like forms although its meat is white and delicate and sweet, weighs up to fourteen pounds, and inhabits the northern half of the Sea of Cortez (composite descriptions from Steinbeck, 1962, p. 155, and Cannon, 1973, p. 263, "Sierra Grande"). Here is where Steinbeck joins the issue of appropriate methodology:

The Mexican sierra has "XVII-15-IX" spines in the dorsal fin. These can easily be counted. But if the sierra strikes hard on the line so that our hands are burned, if the fish sounds and nearly escapes and finally comes in over the rail, his colors pulsing and his tail beating the air, a whole new relational externality has come into being—an entity which is more than the sum of the fish plus the fisherman. The only way to count the spines of the sierra unaffected by this second relational reality is to sit in a laboratory, open an evil-smelling jar, remove a stiff colorless fish from formalin solution, count the spines, and write the truth "D. XVII-15-IX." There you have recorded a reality which cannot be assailed—probably the least important reality concerning either the fish or yourself.

It is good to know what you are doing. The man with his pickled fish has set down one truth and has recorded in his experience many lies. The fish is not that color, that texture, that dead, nor does he smell that way. [pp. 2–3]

I personally think there are many embalmers, picklers, and spine counters among leadership researchers. What worries me is that some of the least important realities about leaders are being accorded some of the largest amounts of attention. I think we need to spend more time watching leaders "on line," whether that line is simulated or real. We have to put ourselves in a better position to watch leaders make do, let it pass, improvise, make inferences, scramble, and all the other things that leaders do during their *days between* more visible moments of glory.

If we resort to that kind of methodological mixture of un-statistical naturalism in the hands of a differentiating generalist (the epitome of scientist as medium), then maybe we will discover two things:

1. Leaders are spineless.
2. Being spineless is a good thing.

If we verified those two things, then we would also be home free in Steinbeck's estimation, because then it would be impossible for us to be spine counters.

References

Ashby, W. R. Self-regulation and requisite variety. In F. D. Emery (Ed.), *Systems thinking*. Baltimore: Penguin, 1969.

Barker, R. G. *Ecological psychology*. Stanford, Calif.: Stanford University Press, 1968.

Bateson, G. *Steps to an ecology of mind*. New York: Ballantine, 1972.

Bateson, M. C. *Our own metaphor*. New York: Knopf, 1972.

Buckley, W. Society as a complex adaptive system. In W. Buckley (Ed.), *Modern systems research for the behavioral scientist*. Chicago: Aldine, 1968.

Cannon, R. *The Sea of Cortez*. Menlo Park, Calif.: Lane, 1973.

Castaneda, C. *Journey to Ixtlan*. New York: Simon and Schuster, 1972.

Dillard, A. *Pilgrim at Tinker Creek*. New York: Bantam, 1975.

Fenichel, O. *The psychoanalytic theory of neuroses*. New York: Norton, 1945.

Glassman, R. B. Persistence and loose coupling in living systems. *Behavioral Science*, 1973, **18**, 83–98.

Goodman, R. A. Environmental knowledge and organizational time horizon: Some functions and dysfunctions. *Human Relations,* 1973, **26**, 215–226.

Heider, F. *The psychology of interpersonal relations.* New York: Wiley, 1958.

Heider, F. Thing and medium. *Psychological Issues,* 1959, **1** (3), 1–34.

Hirschman, A. O., & Lindblom, C. E. Economic development, research and development, policy making: Some converging views. *Behavioral Science,* 1962, **7**, 211–222.

Lifton, R. J. Protean man. *Archives of General Psychiatry,* 1971, **24**, 298–304.

Maccoby, M. A psychoanalytic view of learning. In *Inside academe.* New York: Change Magazine, 1972.

Murphy, G. *Outgrowing self-deception.* New York: Basic Books, 1975.

Murray, H. A. Autobiography. In E. G. Boring & G. Lindzey (Eds.), *A history of psychology in autobiography* (Vol. 5). New York: Appleton-Century-Crofts, 1967.

Pribram, K. A. The new neurology and the biology of emotion: A structural approach. *American Psychologist,* 1967, **22**, 830–838.

Simmel, G. *The sociology of Georg Simmel.* Glencoe, Ill.: Free Press, 1950.

Steinbeck, J. *The log from the Sea of Cortez.* New York: Viking, 1962.

Thomas, L. *The lives of a cell.* New York: Viking, 1974.

Zener, K., & Graffron, M. Perceptual experience: An analysis of its relations to the external world through internal processings. In S. Koch (Ed.), *Psychology: A study of a science* (Vol. 4). New York: McGraw-Hill, 1962.

Zurcher, L. A. The mutable self: An adaptation of accelerated change. *et al.,* 1972, **3** (1), 3–15.

Commentary

Weick's speculation that effective leaders may be good media and use medium characteristics to create desired outcomes in organizations raises several issues relevant to leadership practice and research. One immediate focus is on the set of objects that the leader must perceive. We tend, for example, to look at leadership in terms of recurring, relatively stable patterns. For the leader, however, attention may be focused not on things that are stable but on those that are not stable—on the exceptions and the incongruities (McCall, 1975). Problem solving in organizational leadership roles involves much more than "decision making style." The leader must deal with the sources of the problem, the resources available, individuals, personalities, and time, as well as with finding *a* solution to the problem. How the leader fits all of these parameters together would involve, from Weick's perspective, media qualities: the number of elements available for mediation, independence among the elements, and external as opposed to internal constraints.

Pfeffer argued that leadership may not matter, that environmental constraints severely limit a leader's ability to have an impact. Such an argument partially explains the confusing data on the relationship between leader behavior and group performance: clearly many things other than the leader can influence group outcomes. Weick's point is that a leader who is a good medium is sensitive to these constraints. It is more likely, he suggests, that the individual aware of the causal texture of the environment will have more resources to deal with it and therefore might have more impact on it. The poor medium, seeing only one set of relationships or being completely blind to restraints, cannot hope to effectively use alternative strategies.

Note also that Pfeffer's discussion of attributions to leaders fits into Weick's perspective. The way researchers, subordinates, and organizational members interpret leader behavior depends on their own media qualities. Poor media would erroneously attribute outcomes to a leader by overlooking other explanations. Weick points this out in respect to researchers by describing methods for counting cadavers. His point can be extended to organizational members as well. Subordinates, for example, may be poor media vis-á-vis leaders; this may be one explanation (there are others!) of why there is little agreement between subordinate- and self-perceptions of a leader's style (Jago & Vroom, 1976). Further, training programs that emphasize content may reduce the leader's media qualities. Models are by necessity simplifications of larger phenomena. When a leader is told to focus on X, Y, and Z, he or she is also told not to focus on a wide variety of other events. For researchers the obsession with leadership style has excluded concentration on numerous other components of the leadership process. Training managers to focus on style, even in a contingency framework, may have the same effect.

A major issue raised by Weick's discussion of media and leadership is the apparent contradiction between the docile, malleable stance of a good medium and the active stance of the initiator. This dilemma is certainly not new. Remember the dichotomy often described between "thinkers" and "doers." Weick's conjecture that increased media (passive) qualities also lead to increased action repertoires turns the tables on our usual way of looking at leader qualities. It suggests, for example, that some leaders operate in both active and passive modes—sequentially or even simultaneously. It focuses on cognitive abilities and suggests that the overt behaviors we observe will be contradictory. Unless we understand the content-free processes associated with leadership—in this case, media—we will not be able to make sense of contextually embedded actions. Thus, Pfeffer's point that leadership, at least in some situations, does not matter and Weick's exploration of media qualities intersect at an important question: Under what conditions does leadership count?

Translating Weick's relatively abstract concept into practical research terms is aided by Lundberg's delineation of neglected variables. In the next chapter, he will talk about the self-expectations of leaders, a factor relevant to the medium because it reflects internal constraints. Lundberg will also discuss the leader's shadows, the sounding boards against which leaders can check out their perceptions. Again this reflects "media" behavior in the leadership context.

MWM

References

Jago, A. G., & Vroom, V. H. Perceptions of leadership style: Superior and subordinate descriptions of decision-making behavior. In J. G. Hunt & L. L. Larson (Eds.), *Leadership frontiers*. Kent, Ohio: Kent State University Press, 1976.

McCall, M. W., Jr. Making sense with nonsense: Helping frames of reference clash. In P. C. Nystrom & W. H. Starbuck (Eds.), *Prescriptive models of organizations* (Vol. V). North-Holland/TIMS Studies in the Management Sciences. Amsterdam, The Netherlands: North Holland Publishing Co., 1977.

4. The Unreported Leadership Research of Dr. G. Hypothetical: Six variables in need of recognition

Craig Lundberg

In this essay I wish to report on some of the work of a colleague whose research has often excited me by its unorthodoxy as well as its insight. The work reported below bears more or less on the focus of this conference—leadership. In what follows I attempt to be Professor Hypothetical's Dr. Watson (of Sherlock Holmes' fame). Dr. H's restless brilliance and excessive modesty prohibit him from following through on his researches, for he is impatient with the tedious task of reporting. This, however, is a task I gladly take up for him, so that his inquiries are publicly shared. As Dr. H's chronicler, therefore, I beg your forbearance with these notes. While a confidant and colleague of Dr. H's, I am in no way capable of fully conveying the impact of his person or his research.

The studies to be described are all exploratory. Dr. H's style is to skeptically question, inventively probe, and always remain unfettered by convention, restlessly moving ever forward. His indefatigable curiosity and intellectual pluck have led him to consider leadership among a number of other topics. Knowing this on my invitation to this conference, I decided to confer with him in hopes he might instruct me as he has done so often in the past. Finding him in his study one afternoon, I asked him to help me by telling me what work he had been engaged in. To my delight, he immediately lit his inseparable pipe and settled back, clearly ready to talk. In what follows I have attempted to record, as best I can, his remarks.

"Ah, my friend, you're interested in leadership research. As you know, I've not only been interested in the topic for some years, but actually very concerned about it, too. To be quite candid, I think the proliferation and the nature of contemporary inquiries have been quite misdirected. It's my belief that researchers in the field have become prematurely entranced by a handful of models that may have blinded us to some important variables on the one hand, and on the other hand have prompted an urgency for sophistication as yet unwarranted. My own work has been deliberately different. I don't assume that traditional or popular variables of leadership begin to say it all. Nor do I assume that contemporary models are necessarily adequate or are the only guides for meaningful leadership research. Perhaps you'll better understand these points if I describe some of my own work."

Study the first

"You no doubt recall the demonstration reported by someone in which a class of male students selected a socially isolated female and 'made' her one of the most popular girls on campus. Recall that those young men simply began to speak to her, date her, and talk positively about her. This attention by a group of fellows over time seemingly did something not only to the girl's self-image but also seemingly altered the perceptions of many other males on the campus.

"Well, this demonstration always intrigues students, so in one of my classes we replicated it. The only real change was to reverse the genders, that is, a set of female students of mine selected a young man—and made him 'popular.' Part of the purpose of this class project was to understand the phenomena created. We came up with all sorts of alternative 'explanations' in terms of reference groups, conformity, conditioning, dissonance, and so forth. Later, as I thought about it, however, I began to wonder if the notion of 'self-expectation' wasn't a more parsimonious way of comprehending what had happened. My thinking went like this: Regardless of the social mechanisms operating, they probably impacted the focal person's view of himself, so that over time his self-expectations regarding his popularity were altered in a more positive way.

"Now, this line of reasoning prompted me to recall some things

I'd read over the years. I remembered that Rosenthal (1966, 1973) had shown that expectations are significant factors in such disparate settings as education and psychological research, and that Livingston (1969), and King (1974), and Lundberg (1975) reported that managerial expectations account for a sizable proportion of worker behavior. I also recalled that while expectations have been looked at in leadership studies, the focus has been on the expectations of others, not the leader (Stogdill, 1974). Well, I thought to myself, why not extend this line of research to investigating the effects of self-expectations on leadership.

"You'll perhaps remember that I did a little laboratory experiment on this. My hypothesis was simply that group members in leaderless problem-solving teams would tend to select as leader that member who had positive self-expectations of his own leadership capabilities. At the time I was influenced by Wiggens (1968), who argues that a relatively weak manipulation of the independent variable shows its impact more decisively.

"First, I got twelve teams of five unacquainted students to come to my laboratory. When a team arrived, my assistant put them into separate rooms to fill out a longish questionnaire containing mostly blind items. Only two standard items asked for self-estimates of the student's leadership capability. My assistant then collected the questionnaires, and he and I conveniently stood within overhearing distance of one randomly chosen member. I said that the member had, on the basis of the questionnaire, 'definite leadership potential.' That, you see, was the experimental manipulation. Anyhow, the team was then collected, put in a conference room, and instructed that they had twenty minutes to discuss a problem and come to a consensus. At the end of this problem-solving time, we sent the team back to their own separate rooms to fill out a post-questionnaire. Again this was sort of long, again all blind items except for one, asking for a ranking of the 'leadership' provided by each member's fellow team members.

"From what I've sketched, you can see that the independent variable was 'self-expectation of leadership capability,' and the dependent variable was operationalized as 'perceived leadership.' My hope, of course, was that the member who overheard me would thereby develop a positive self-expectation of his leadership capability, that this would show up in his behavior in the problem-solving session, and that this would be noticed by his teammates. I thought that if I got any ranking of the focal member greater than chance, then my implanted self-expectation was accounting for it. Well, that's what happened. Not a very strong effect to be sure, but I had set it up so that any effect at all was promising. All I can say is that those leadership research types ought to introduce self-expectation into their models, probably as an intervening variable. I've believed for a long time that this whole 'pygmalion' business is underrated by most scholars, and I now know it to be so for leadership."

Study the second

"Let's see now, what else have I learned about leadership? Let me now remind you about the MBA student club that was started here a few years ago. It was some reflective thought about that that got me into another study. The young man who initiated the idea for the club and who was subsequently elected its first president was Jerry. Jerry was a high-energy, outgoing sort of chap who really threw himself into the establishment of the club. In the second year, however, Jerry wasn't reelected; rather it was Doug. Doug was the quiet type. Oh, capable enough, and motivated enough, but not dynamic at all. Somehow the ordering of those two presidents seemed right, the high-energy, dynamic chap during the organizational start-up, the quieter chap to administer the club. While no doubt lots of factors were operating, it was the difference in the expressed energy levels of the two men that really struck me.

"I began to wonder about this energy level stuff and leadership. First, as is my habit, I went to the literature—and quickly came up with activation/arousal as something really ignored. Early interest in activation was prompted by Duffy (1951, 1962), Lindsley (1951, pp. 473–516), and Fiske and Maddi (1961). It was the work of Berlyne (1960), however, that really got me going. If the level of experienced stimuli can predict the activity level (from a minimum in sleep or unconsciousness to a maximum as in elation or intense anger), then the leadership literature again was probably missing some important stuff.

"In digging into my files, I found two pieces of work that seemed to confirm these impressions. The first was Scott's paper

(1966) in which he used activation theory to better explain that old problem we call performance decline. As a person becomes familiar with his surroundings and task, there will be a habituation in the brain stem reticular formation leading to a decrement in performance. If the person cannot increase the stimuli impact, the result is a continuous decline in performance. The second piece of work that got me going was your working paper (Lundberg, 1974), in which you showed that worker performance varied with the combined stimuli of task and supervision. Specifically, I was intrigued with your reinterpretation of some of the older case studies in activation terms. I asked myself if what you had reported could be analogous for managers and other leaders. Well, the two successive MBA club presidents and the activation literature suggested all sorts of projects to my mind. Let me tell you about one exploratory study I conducted as a sample of how this line of investigation can go.

"You'll recall that the range of acceptable/normal stimuli for a person is technically called 'tonus.' My working hypothesis was that successful leaders are those persons whose own tonus requires the initiation of activities that are congruent with the stimuli requirements of the group. That is, since the tasks will provide a certain level of stimuli, the preferred leader will be one who supplies additional stimuli so that the total doesn't exceed or go below the average tonus level of the group. For the study I'm about to describe, I'm simply reversing the perspective you were using. Whereas you asked what was the effect on productivity of various combinations of task and supervisor stimuli, I asked—given various levels of task stimuli—which leaders would be perceived as effective if they varied in the amounts of stimuli they provided?

"This study was designed as a very simple experiment. I devised two levels of task stimuli conditions and two levels of leadership behavior, providing a two by two design. It looks like Figure 1.

"What happened went like this: A small team was brought into the laboratory, given either a difficult, demanding task or a very routine, boring task and permitted to practice a while. At the beginning of the work period, a confederate appeared, called himself leader, and proceeded to initiate the work and manage it. These confederates were carefully 'programmed' to behave in one

Task Conditions

		Hi stimuli	Lo stimuli
Leadership	Hi stimuli	A	B
Activity			
Levels	Lo stimuli	C	D

Figure 1

of two ways—either to be very, very active in talking with the group or to be very quiet, even laissez-faire. You can now see that I predicted that the group in cells A and D would be over- and under-stimulated, respectively, and that the leaders of those treatments would be rated as ineffective. By the way, all groups had been 'averaged' as to their members' tonus level. The leader effectiveness rating, of course, occurred in a questionnaire administered post-experimentally. My predictions were confirmed as you might have anticipated.

"You may be wondering what that study had to do with Jerry and Doug. This relates to a follow-up study that generally replicated the above, but without confederates. There I composed unacquainted groups and watched for emerging leaders—hunching as in the case of Jerry and Doug that the leaders who would emerge would be those who either provided the additional necessary social stimuli or buffered excessive task stimuli. Of interest in this second project was how task and social leadership styles worked. But you can speculate on that. You might suggest at your conference that activation is a promising way to sum variables in contingency models, for it is used as an intervening variable. Let's walk over to the store so I can get some tobacco, and on the way I'll tell you about some other leadership studies I've done."

Study the third

"Since you've not only been attentive but seem relatively open to hearing about my work, let me relate some of my experiences that eventually led to some rather odd leadership research. I suppose it all began the summer I went to participate in a sensitivity training group. You may remember, my young friend, how you teased me for being skeptical about such 'groups' when I hadn't ever seen one. Well, my wife and I did go on our summer vacation to a N.T.L. laboratory (so-called). It was up in the mountains and was for two weeks. Actually, there were several separate groups going simultaneously. Anyhow, after several days, I saw an announcement posted that offered participants the chance to meditate each morning, before breakfast and before the group sessions began. Having no experience with meditation either, I joined these volunteers and 'sat' each morning for the rest of the lab. I found it to be a refreshing way to start the day; every day I seemed to achieve more and more 'inner stillness' and most surprisingly also seemed to stay more focused in the 'here and now' while in the T-group. (Forgive the jargon; you know my penchant for it.) I came away not only with a respect for what can be learned in those kinds of groups but also quite impressed with the benefits of meditation.

"Soon after these experiences, I joined with a young psychologist to offer an executive seminar. One evening over drinks, my friend, who is intellectually fascinated with individual decision making, and I chatted about what contributes to effective executive performance. We talked our way to this shared belief—the less distractable an executive, the more likely his decision making will be effective. This, as you see, is a twist on the old caveat that a decision maker must have all the facts; we were saying, in effect, that being able to focus on the facts is equally important.

"I relate these two seemingly unconnected experiences because they prompted a series of leadership studies. The first step in this series was to confirm my personal experience with meditation and T-group. I found in my own region a similar laboratory that was well staffed and had multiple groups. I talked the director into permitting me to offer some simple zazen meditation (oh, yes, I had gotten some expertise) to half the groups, to pre- and posttest all participants in terms of their training, and to have graduate students observe each group. At the end of each day I also got a crude measure of individual anxiety level by means of the Zuckerman and Lubin check list (1965). The results confirmed my own experience—members of groups who regularly meditated experienced less anxiety and increased learning. While all of that was interesting, it did leave me with the question of whether this 'inner stilling' technique was applicable to task or work groups.

"Thus, I designed a follow-up study. I was about to get involved in a lot of training of the nominal group technique (Delbecq & Van de Ven, 1971) and saw the opportunity to test the utility of meditation there. This work was with many, many teams in our state's public agencies. On a voluntary basis, therefore, I invited some of these teams to meditate with me prior to our training each day. A colleague was already conducting an evaluation study of training effectiveness, so I merely tacked on a couple of items to his pre-, immediate post-, and later instruments. While the findings were possibly confounded in several ways, once more the meditation seemed to have the expected effect. Namely, those teams who had meditated seemed to acquire the nominal group technique more quickly and use it more effectively. However, the next question that occurred to me was whether or how meditation might enhance leadership. Since this question was closer to my professional heart, I then designed three small research studies to see what I could learn.

"The first project in the series was exceedingly simple. I had access to several classes at my school that routinely used team projects. At the beginning of the term, once teams had been formed and team leaders chosen, I invited approximately half of these leaders to meditate with me late each afternoon (a convenient time to meet, although the teams met at all hours). I had already arranged with the course instructors to get *weekly* team member perceptions of their leader's behavior—using part of an instrument that resembled a 'post-meeting response form.' From these weekly samplings, I was able to chart the perceptions of leaders who had meditated against those who hadn't. Again, the lack of standardization of teams, operating procedures, leader styles, and a host of other variables make the findings rather suspect, but it was consistent with some parallel work of Lesh (1970) with counselors. Since there were observable differences, however, I felt that once more this somewhat 'kooky' device of meditation was significant enough to continue my researches.

"The second project was more formally conceived. Here I was

able to assemble a large number of small (six-member) groups and insure reasonable intergroup comparability. These were designated leaderless teams who had the task of meeting three days a week for six consecutive weeks to discuss a series of management 'cases.' Using considerable charm and persuasion, I convinced two members of each team to 'sit' with me in meditation (you see I had already some reputation in my school for this) each day before teams met. Some artfulness was required to keep the rather special membership of this 'meditation class' from being known by other team members (this was accomplished mostly by inviting lots of other students in to meditate, too). Since I was ultimately interested in whether, other things being more or less equal, the students doing meditation would be more often perceived as contributing leadership to their teams than would their peers, after each week I had all participants respond to this question among many others: 'Name the member of your team who, this week, has provided the most effective leadership to your team.' Without boring you with the details, my friend, let me smugly say that by the end of the sixth week, the only members named, with the exception of one, were meditators. Having now confirmed for myself that the effects of meditation produced leader-like behaviors, I turned to the crucial last study in this series.

"What still bothered me about this nondistraction training (through meditation) was how it might affect real managers in actual administrative leadership situations. For years now I've lectured about the 'complementary' model of leadership, where the effective leader fulfills the leadership functions not performed by group members. I believed that a stronger test of my nondistractable thesis (namely that nondistracted or inner-stilled leaders make better decisions because they can focus better on the facts) would occur if actual managers widened their repertoire of leadership behaviors in practice in association with meditation. As it so happened, not too much later I found myself once more forced into consulting to augment my income. It was fortuitous that I was asked to consult with a number of district managers in two regions of a major business firm. Seeing the research opportunity, I negotiated permission to involve my students in the project. What I did was to train several graduate assistants to observe managers on the job, acquiring five-minute samples of behavior in accordance with a coding scheme derived from Mintzberg's (1973) work (this helped my coaching of the managers, earned my high consultant fees, and provided data on managerial repertoires for my research purposes). All relevant managers in the two regions were observed for three days each. My student assistants then gained valuable insights by processing these data. I then held a two-day 'training' session of a typical sort for these managers. (In my opinion, training does little for the participants but clearly gets top management endorsement.) A second one-day follow-up session was held with the managers of one region. It was during this day that I introduced meditation. By this time I could easily rationalize this unusual training technique by mentioning the nondistractability reasoning. Eliciting their promise to continue daily meditation for three weeks and then report on its effects, I left satisfied that my charisma and reasoning had convinced them to really do the meditation.

"My graduate students were sent back to the field in the third week to observe for one day, confirming that most of the managers in the region in fact were meditating. These student observers also repeated their observing of all relevant managers in both regions one month later. Clearly, what I wanted to learn was whether the repertoires of the managers exposed to meditation had in fact increased and, if so, in what way.

"Now out of this project I learned two things—that managerial repertoires did widen, and that these managers reported better mental health in general and more focused clarity in problem solving in particular. I know, I know, young friend, you're wondering if I hadn't once again planted expectations; or if the meditation had only altered their arousal levels, or, heaven forbid, that the conventional training had 'taken' somehow. To tell you the truth, I can't be positive those sorts of things didn't occur. Yet my unerring sense is that nondistractability does enhance leader capabilities. Someday, perhaps, I'll write for a grant to adequately replicate my field study in the laboratory.

"Have I been telling you anything that may be useful to you? You think so? Good. My hope, of course, is to infect you with the provocation and urgency I've felt about the state of leadership research. Let me suggest we rendezvous tomorrow afternoon at my club where we may continue this conversation."

Study the fourth

"Ah, good afternoon. Here, let me order you a sherry, the only fit beverage for a serious thinker. There, now where were we? As I recall, I was describing to you several of my leadership studies. Let me commence this afternoon by mentioning a little project that relates even more to the body than the activation work I spoke of yesterday.

"The story of this study began quite remarkably. My wife had, after our T-group experiences, taken up with the local growth center. For my birthday, she gave me a gift of a 'rolfing' session. Now let me quickly explain that rolfing is a deep massage that so affects the musculature that the body achieves a natural realignment. Anyhow, I went. You know my curiosity. It was something!

"First, it was rather painful. The rolfer more than massaged; she actually ran her fingers under my long muscles and pulled the adhesions loose. And the rolfer not only was a woman, but looked fifteen years younger than her age of sixty—and she was as strong and pliable as someone half her age. But I digress. After the session I felt renewed in ways I'm not able to adequately describe. On returning to the office (I was filling in for the department chairman at the time), I was confronted with two crises. In the next few hours I handled both problems with an ease and dispatch unequalled in my past experience as an administrator.

"This last experience prompted some investigation on my part into the theoretical basis of rolfing. I soon found that Reich's (1961) theory of 'armoring' was behind not only rolfing and structural reintegration but also Lowen's (1958) bioenergetics and a whole school of psychotherapy reported in the *Journal of Orgonomy*. Armoring refers to chronic muscular tension that captures, in the body, character difficulties of the person. We all easily recognize this in extreme cases; just think of Casper Milquetoast and his perpetual stoop of acquiescence. The more I read, the more I thought someone should look into the relation of this body armoring to leader behavior.

	Initial Leadership Situation	Experimental Intervention	Second Leadership Situation
Experimental Groups		"rolfing"	
Control Groups A		//////	
Control Groups B	//////	//////	

Figure 2

"Well, with my enthusiasm, I soon designed a study to check the correlations, if any, between leader success and armoring. I decided that since this whole notion was so uncommon I'd better do a rather careful study. My design looked like Figure 2.

"With this design, I believed any effect of carefully matched groups' body alteration would show up. The initial leadership situation was a standard one, with the leaders selected randomly, of course. During this period each group was observed; and immediately after, the members rated their leader. The leaders in the experimental groups were then provided with three rolfing sessions apiece. The second leadership situation was functionally equivalent to the first, as well as observed and evaluated identically.

"Remember what was behind this work. The reasoning goes like this: Armoring prohibits the free flow of energy in the organism, and armoring also means character problems implying less sensitivity to one's situation. Rolfing, by reducing a leader's armoring, would permit him not only to more perceptively note the needs and wants of group members, but also to behave more appropriately in response to them. Now if something even remotely resembling this happens, it's mighty important to know about, especially for leaders.

"Now, as you no doubt have anticipated, getting those randomly selected group leaders to go along with the rolfing was rather awkward. In fact, this was the flaw in my design. While some rolfed leaders did in fact improve, some didn't at all. So, while the general idea of the study was confirmed, the finding that I want to pursue is why reducing the armoring of people who didn't want it was not effective. But since I'm in the middle of this at the present, I'll have to save it for another day. Let's have another sherry, and I'll tell you about some other studies."

Study the fifth

"Over the years as I've consulted with managers, I've noticed, as many others have, that the higher up in the hierarchy a manager rises, the more socially isolated he becomes. Yet among top executives, some seem not only to survive but to actually thrive. This puzzled me for years, though I confess I really didn't think much about it. Then last year one of our colleagues, the one who does what he calls Organizational Development, happened to mention he was acting as a 'shadow consultant' (Schroder, 1974). On inquiring just what this was, I was told that a shadow consultant was the person that a consultant checked with periodically for personal support and professional assessment of his role, tactics, diagnoses, etc. This clicked not only for me personally, but permitted me to hypothesize about the isolated executives. My hunch broadly was: High-ranking managers who select and use the equivalent of a shadow consultant would more likely, other things being equal, be more competent as organizational leaders.

"While intriguing, this hunch was fraught with difficulties in testing. Finding an appropriate sample of managers, comparing their settings and work to normalize them, getting an accurate reading on their use of 'shadow leaders,' etc., are major problems for any field study, the sort of research that is most telling. Thus, I chose to go forward with this project with a two-step strategy. First, I needed to confirm whether my hunch was viable; hence, I began to simply pay calls on those executives already in my acquaintance. With these persons I had a crude sense of their job situations and their general reputation for successful leadership. In informal interviews, then, I probed their use of shadow leaders. It didn't take too long for me to conclude that the more successful managers did tend to use shadow leaders, but that there were a wide variety of others and that a variety of topics were, in fact, discussed with them. Since I felt I was on to something, I decided to switch to a more formalized study.

"As usual, hampered by funding, I turned to my school and

students. This project actually was quite simply conceived. I selected a large undergraduate class, using a one-semester, complex computer simulation in which student teams formed firms in a competitive industry. As team leaders, I assigned first-year graduate students. From a second-year graduate class, a set of 'consultants' was designated. Now these consultants not only had competency to advise on the technical aspects of the simulation, they also had counseling skills. The team leaders were told they could draw on these consultants in any way they wanted, whenever they wanted. These consultants, of course, were the key to my research. They kept accurate records on the number, length, and content of all interactions with leaders. They were coached to be responsive on any sort of topic initiated from technical to personal matters. I also invited these consultants to use me if I could be of help in any way. Note, there were two opportunities to investigate the use of shadow leaders: one as leaders used consultants, the other as the consultants used me. Oh yes, both leaders and consultants kept a diary, too. Interesting was the use of 'shadows' mostly when leaders/consultants were doing either very poorly or very well, this finding clearly conditioned by the degree to which the leader/consultant was socially integrated with his team/client. For example, if a leader was somewhat aloof from his team, he tended to use a consultant for task and personal reasons if his team wasn't doing so well, and mostly for personal reasons if the team was doing well. Most personal-social relating, however, was initiated in the guise of technical requests.

"While this may be a minor factor in the larger picture of leadership, I was motivated to do this work because what passes for leadership 'theory' seems relatively inapplicable to institutional leaders, persons leading large, purposive systems. In fact, there is much to be done in this regard. Why don't you get involved? For instance, study the symbolic functions of leadership (suggested by Pandarus' [1973] contention that in academic organizations the leader must exhibit 'symbolicness'), the conceptual competency of leaders and what difference this makes, the whole area of conflict management and leadership at the top, and so on. My point is that leadership research foci could be derived usefully from top managers and would be a lot more pertinent to them. To drive this home, recall your own theme that managers are essentially political creatures; yet who has followed up on Seligman's (1968) urging to study the politics of leadership?"

Study the sixth

"Talking of organizational leaders and their coalitions reminds me of another study you may be interested in. It all got started as I reviewed some older social-psychological literature. Asch's (1958) classic study on the effects of group pressure on the modification of judgments was one such item. I was impressed anew by the power that the presence of a true partner has had in keeping a group member from being a 'yielder.' Another paper was Harvey and Consalvi's (1960) in which they reported that the second highest status member in a small group was more conforming to the group than either the leader or those lower in status. Well, these illustrate what was catching my eye, namely, for teams or groups with leaders, the impact of the leader's coalitions—especially the selection, and the use and effect of 'lieutenants' by leaders.

"It occurred to me that leaders make rather crucial choices in who become their lieutenants. Whether undertaken formally or informally, formation of these coalitions should be with others (a) who themselves have a wide and powerful set of followers, and (b) who complement the competencies of the leaders—at least those were my initial suppositions. Then the problem became how to study this phenomena. The truth is that while compulsively driven to investigate these matters, I had little time or energy to do so. Therefore, I chose to do a quick and dirty pilot study, intending to follow up with a more substantial project.

"I had at hand managers in a summer executive development program. My procedure went as follows. Each manager was given a battery of tests, feedback from which enabled him to get in touch with his own capabilities. Then each manager was given data about the members of a team (these data included demographic, educational, experiential, sociometric, and other information). The manager was then given detailed descriptions of two group tasks—one crisis-like, the other reflecting routine conditions. The manager was then told he was going to be in charge of the team that would actually do the two tasks. He was instructed to select an 'assistant' from among the team members. Since all managers had been chosen to attend the executive program because they had been successful and were in line for a top management promotion, I assumed they were all reasonably 'effective,' and if their selection of assistants was in accordance with my suppositions, I would have initial confirmation. This did happen rather markedly, but one other criterion for selection was mentioned consistently, too, one I should have thought of—the perceived energy level of people, which is a criterion I find myself using, too."

Studies in general

"Let me muse aloud now about this sample of my work and where I see leadership research as being and where it should be going. You'll note that my own work is clearly outside the purview of normal leadership research. It's my belief that today we are getting locked into a set of leadership models and their testing. Whether it's path goal, expectancy, discrepancy, or contingency, it's as if these models somehow adequately define the conceptual territory. It's time, in my opinion and that of Korman (1974), to break loose from this 'strangulation.' Either step back and attempt to integrate our existing knowledge—Halal's (1974) recent effort is an example of what I mean—or give up the term leadership altogether and move back to managing as also suggested by Weick (1974). To be sure, my work is defective in many ways. The measurement is shoddy. Although if I had had multiple criteria of leader effectiveness, I would forgive myself. Similarly, I have not given enough credence to situational variables, a point correctly noted by Fleishman (1973). Also, none of my studies was longitudinal, a defect shared with almost all of the literature. It's high time someone invested in counteracting the static view of leadership that short time research implies. To paraphrase Max Otto (1949), much trouble might have been saved had the noun leadership never come into use, had everyone learned to use instead a verb like leadering or leadered. We are all in the habit of believing that a state corresponding to every noun in the language must somehow exist.

"So what have these studies quietly proclaimed? I think I show

how interesting work can be done inexpensively with what's at hand. I've avoided using many established 'leadership' concepts and measures, i.e., LPC or consideration and structure, in favor of letting my fancy and my experiences lead me. You see, for some time I've been acting on the thoughts you (Lundberg, 1976) recently put down, that contemporary researchers in our field have placed undue emphasis on hypothesis testing as opposed to hypothesis generation. It seems to me that my work has exemplified some other desirable features, too. For example, the very early focus on the personality factors of leaders that gave way to a situational appropriateness view is being reinstated, and my studies on armoring and distractability, I think, show how trait factors might be supplanted with physiological and psychophysical variables. The investigations on activation and self-expectations also show the way, if crudely, toward intervening variables, a very necessary development for future leadership research. Actually, the directionality in most causal models is pretty suspect to my mind, better bi-directionality, better yet sticking to prediction correlational designs—after all, causality is not very defensible in behavioral science at all. The last point I would make is to get leadership research back in the field to make it more relevant to administrative behavior. My work on shadow leaders and leader coalitions are examples of that point in useful directions.

"You want to know what is next on my schedule of leadership research? Well, my hunch is that we'll clarify a lot of what we now know when we bring task and technology into our work. These fundamental notions have been ignored long enough in organizational behavior generally, and somehow I can't escape the belief that what leaders do in their normal work makes one heck of a lot of difference to their leading.

"It's getting a little late and I have to be going. My wife and I are going to a concert tonight. I hope that you've seen, as I think I have, that leadership is an area of research full of challenges. More important, I hope you've heard my concern that leadership researchers try some new variables, and try them playfully— after all, my middle name isn't Galumphus[1] for nothing. Oh yes,

1. Galumphing, according to Miller (1973), is the enhancement of learning by the playful complication of familiar performances.

you ought to come to the concert tonight for there is going to be a marvelous opportunity to observe leadership—imagine the conductor of our little symphony when Alice Cooper is the guest artist."

References

Asch, S. E. Effects of group pressure upon the modification and distortion of judgments. In E. Maccoby, T. Newcomb, & E. Hartly (Eds.), *Readings in social psychology*. New York: Holt, 1958.

Berlyne, D. E. *Conflict, arousal and curiosity*. New York: McGraw-Hill, 1960.

Delbecq, A., & Van De Ven, A. H. A group process model for problem identification and program planning. *Journal of Applied Behavioral Science*, 1971, **7**, 466–492.

Duffy, E. The concept of energy mobilization. *Psychological Review*, 1951, **58**, 30–40.

Duffy, E. *Activation behavior*. New York: Wiley, 1962.

Fiske, D., & Maddi, S. *Functions of varied experience*. Homewood, Ill.: Dorsey, 1961.

Fleishman, E. Overview. In E. A. Fleishman & J. G. Hunt (Eds.), *Current developments in the study of leadership*. Carbondale: Southern Illinois University Press, 1973.

Halal, W. Toward a general theory of leadership. *Human Relations*, 1974, **27**, 401–416.

Harvey, O. J., & Consalvi, C. Status and conformity to pressures in informal groups. *Journal of Abnormal and Social Psychology*, 1960, **60**, 182–187.

King, A. Expectation effects in organizational change. *Administrative Science Quarterly*, 1974, **19**, 221–230.

Korman, A. Contingency approaches to leadership: An overview. In J. G. Hunt & L. Larson (Eds.), *Contingency approaches to leadership*. Carbondale: Southern Illinois University Press, 1974.

Lesh, T. Zen meditation and the development of empathy in counselors. *Journal of Humanistic Psychology*, 1970, **10**, 39–74.

Lindsley, D. B. Emotion. In S. S. Stevens (Ed.), *Handbook of experimental psychology*. New York: Wiley, 1951.

Livingston, J. S. Pygmalion in management. *Harvard Business Review*, 1969, **47**(4), 81–89.

Lowen, A. *Physical dynamics of character structure*. New York: Grune and Stratton, 1958.

Lundberg, C. *An experiment relating management style and task complexity to performance and satisfaction: Activation as an intervening variable*. Paper presented at the meeting of the Western Academy of Management, San Francisco, 1974.

Lundberg, C. The effect of managerial expectation and task scope on team productivity and satisfaction: A laboratory study. *Journal of Business Research*, 1975, 3(3), 189–197.

Lundberg, C. Hypothesis creation in organizational behavior research. *Academy of Management Review*, 1976, 1(2), 5–12.

Miller, S. Ends, means, galumphing: Some leitmotifs of play. *American Anthropologist*, 1973, 75(1), 87–98.

Mintzberg, H. *The nature of managerial work*. New York: Harper and Row, 1973.

Otto, M. *Science and the moral life*. New York: Mentor, 1949.

Pandarus. One's own primer of academic politics. *The American Scholar*, 1973, 42, 569–592.

Reich, W. *The function of the orgasm*. New York: Farrar, Straus & Giroux, 1961.

Rosenthal, R. *Experimenter effects in behavioral research*. New York: Appleton-Century-Crofts, 1966.

Rosenthal, R. The Pygmalion effect lives. *Psychology Today*, September 1973, pp. 56–63.

Scott, W. E. Activation theory and task design. *Organizational Behavior and Human Performance*, 1966, 1, 3–30.

Seligman, L. Leadership: Political aspects. In D. Sills (Ed.), *International encyclopedia of the social sciences*. New York: Macmillan, 1968.

Shroder, M. The shadow consultant. *Journal of Applied Behavioral Science*, 1974, 10, 579–594.

Stogdill, R. *Handbook of leadership*. New York: Free Press, 1974.

Weick, K. Review essay: Henry Mintzberg, the nature of managerial work. *Administrative Science Quarterly*, 1974, 19, 111–118.

Wiggens, J. A. Hypothesis validity and experimental laboratory methods. In H. M. Blalock & A. B. Blalock (Eds.), *Methodology in social research*. New York: McGraw-Hill, 1968.

Zuckerman, J., & Lubin, B. *Multiple Affect Adjective Checklist: Manual*. Princeton, N.J.: Educational Testing Service, 1965.

Commentary

Lundberg's six neglected variables—self-expectation, activity level, distractability, body armoring, shadows, and coalitions—represent an array of research foci ranging from individual to group centered, from physical through personal to behavioral. Four of the six seem particularly fruitful for leadership research. Self-expectation as a leadership variable is related to self-motivation. Whereas most studies of leadership have focused on the expectations and motivations of subordinates vis-á-vis the leader, Lundberg points out the leader's own internal states (largely conditioned by outside forces including the subordinates) are an important part of the leadership process. Brim (1975) has suggested that self-perception of one's ability to change is an important factor in career development, and this idea fits well with the thrust of Lundberg's arguments about leadership. Failure of personality traits to predict leadership success may have led researchers to prematurely switch emphasis to behavior. Non-trait internal states—states that can and often do change with environmental and structural changes—no doubt contribute to leadership behavior. This suggests that other social-psychological processes, such as dissonance reduction, attribution, and aggression, might help us understand the behavior and attitudes of leaders.

Activity level, particularly Lundberg's notion of stimuli manipulation, is related to Weick's description of the leader as medium. In Lundberg's sense, the amount of stimulus a leader should provide subordinates is related to the task and to the activity level of the group. Notice that activity-level stimuli are content free. By focusing at a content-free level, the research is forced into a process mode. In this context the verb "leadering" makes more sense than the noun "leader" and the search for an invariant "one best" leadership style for each situation becomes irrelevant.

Shadows and lieutenants, other dimensions of leadership addressed by Lundberg, also hold promise for understanding leadership processes. They suggest an informal and formal mechanism for getting the job done. Coalition formation is normally viewed as a process of obtaining power, but Lundberg points out that it is also a process of extending competency. Since individuals in leadership roles engage in numerous activities, are bombarded with information, and must deal with numerous role sets, coalitions of leader-followers-peers make sense in non-political, goal-centered contexts. In Lundberg's framework, delegation is not simply a leadership style but, more broadly, a political and practical tool for dealing with complex realities.

Lundberg not only suggests some neglected personal and interpersonal variables, but also describes some simple research designs for testing their potential. The style of playful conjecture coupled with empirical exploration suggests one way of expanding the conceptual arena of leadership. Weick's differentiated generalist is another alternative.

In the next chapter Pondy will elaborate the conceptual expansion theme by dealing with the meaning of the word "leadership" and examining frameworks that have been applied to linguistics and might be useful in leadership. His suggestion that language itself is part of the leadership process provides additional insight into Weick's development of the leader as medium.

MWM

Reference

Brim, O. G., Jr. *Life span development of the theory of oneself.* Invited address to the International Society for the Study of Behavioural Development Biennial Conference, University of Surrey, Guildford, Surrey, England, July 1975.

5. Leadership Is a Language Game

Louis R. Pondy

Let me begin by sharing with you some doubts and impressions about the field of leadership.

1. Most people would agree, I think, that leadership is a form of social influence. But then so are most things that involve more than one person (e.g., social facilitation effects, group decision making). So have we solved anything by that categorization? I suppose it does exclude a few things (e.g., leadership as a personality trait), but not much, it seems to me. Perhaps it would help to say that by the term "leadership" we mean social (i.e., interpersonal) influence exercised by a person in some position of superior authority (leaving aside for the time being the source of the authority) over some subordinate.

But, of course, we all recognize that there are "informal" leaders; that is, people who exercise influence over group members without occupying any formally recognized slot. And informal leaders are so common that restricting the term "leadership" to something done by persons in formal leadership positions seems a bit silly. In any case, I entertain doubts as to whether thinking of leadership as a type of social influence is very helpful, although at the present moment I cannot present any viable alternatives.

2. Leadership is applied to a pastiche of behaviors, ranging from that of foreman to that of prophet. It seems unlikely to me that we understand those behaviors well enough to identify the elements common to all. George Graen has mentioned to me that while his Vertical Dyad Linkage model (Dansereau, Graen, & Haga, 1975) seemed to fit "administrative supervisors" reasonably well, the Ohio State data on "foremen" fit it much more poorly.

And I think of foremen and administrative supervisors as being conceptually adjacent! Have we been misled by the existence of a single term in our language to think that it reflects some uniform reality? Gregory Bateson (1972) has argued that our language is thing-oriented and is impoverished when it comes to thinking about, describing, and talking about relationships. Eskimos have seven different names for snow because they are so familiar with it. Does our insistence on the single term "leadership" say something about our familiarity or experience with it?

3. *A closely related point: Our epistemology seems to force us to agree on a conceptual definition of the term "leadership."* But Ian Mitroff has been urging on us some alternative inquiring strategies that stress eclecticism and dialecticism in place of agreement (see, for example, Mitroff & Pondy, 1974). Now surely there have been a multitude of conceptual schemes for describing leadership, but it seems to me that they have been operating independently with occasional attempts to identify, say, a low LPC score with initiating structure and with a directive leadership style (more on the question of "style" later).

Perhaps what I am suggesting here is that we not only disaggregate leadership conceptually (as suggested in point 2), but that we attempt to fully account for the diversity and divergence of interacting explanations. In other words, the current conceptual schemes are not different enough. They overlap one another too easily. We are getting dense coverage of too limited an area. To one who believes in a consensus epistemology, that would be a signal for celebration, a sure symptom that we are converging on a solution. But is it perhaps a precise solution to the wrong problem? With a style of inquiry that stresses consensus, we have no way of knowing whether we have converged on a local rather than a global optimum—a correct solution to the wrong problem. So, in both this point and the prior one, I am arguing for more variety in the way we think about leadership and in what we think of as leadership.

4. *I find the concept of leadership "style" particularly disturbing.* It connotes to me superficiality of action, without either sincerity of intent or substantive meaning. My guess is that early research-

ers on leadership style meant to say something about the whole manner in which the leader approached his task, including his attitudes and values, and that the research on democratic styles of leadership was a reaction on a very fundamental level to the excesses of totalitarian regimes. But somewhere along the line we lost sight of the "deep structure" or meaning of leadership style, and I see it being taught to and practiced by students only at the level of "surface structure," that is, only at the level of superficial expression. The terms deep and surface structure derive from the field of linguistics (e.g., Chomsky, 1972), and perhaps it would be worthwhile to take a small detour to explain how they are used there.

Very briefly, grammar is the relation between sound and meaning. In turn, grammar can be decomposed into phonetics, syntactics, and semantics. A phonetic representation (the surface structure of an expression) is what we ordinarily recognize as a string of words comprising a sentence, and phonetics is the study of the relation between sound and its phonetic representation. Semantics studies the relation between meaning and its semantic representation or deep structure, a set of primitive statements or expressions. Syntactics is the study of the relation between phonetic and semantic representations. To speak a language is to be master of all three components of grammar. Now back to leadership.

Suppose we think of leadership as a language. To practice, say, democratic leadership is to understand the set of meanings (values?) to be conveyed, to give them primitive expression, to translate them into stylistic representations, and ultimately to choose sounds and actions that manifest them. My worry is that this overarching process has been truncated, and that we have reduced the grammar of leadership to its phonetics. The syntactics and especially the semantics of leadership have been lost sight of. One particular conjecture about the source of this loss haunts me: Sounds, actions, and surface expressions are observable; they constitute behavior that can be "scientifically" measured in a reproducible way. But deep structures, and especially meanings, are elusive concepts that have no physical, behavioral counterpart. They cannot be observed. But if leadership is to be studied scientifically, attention must therefore be limited to the observable, surface, stylistic components. I reject the epistemology implicit in this conjecture on both scientific and ethical grounds. Perhaps I have overdrawn the parallel between leadership and linguistics, but I do not think so.

5. *Nearly all theories of leadership identify only a small number of strategies to choose from.* You can use either a democratic, autocratic, or laissez-faire style. You can emphasize either consideration or initiating structure. Or if you really want to get fancy, Vroom and Yetton (1973) offer *six* different things you can do. Now there is something profoundly troubling about this. Invariably when I have attempted to teach extant leadership theories, especially to practicing managers, they have bridled under the constraints imposed by so few alternative ways of behaving. I believe that we have sacrificed the creative aspect of leadership for its programmatic aspects. Shouldn't we be trying to document the *variety* of leadership strategies, rather than trying to collapse it into a few constraining categories?

A lesson from linguistics is relevant here again. What is truly remarkable about language is its creative aspect. Virtually all utterances are novel—never before spoken. And even young children and intellectually subnormal people have the capacity to produce creative sentences. Since there is no limit to the length of the longest sentence, there is an unbounded (infinite?) number of possible sentences in a given language. And the problem of linguistics is to describe how this infinite set of sentences is produced and interpreted with our *finite* (!) brain capacities. In fact, Chomsky defines the explanation of this creative aspect as the core problem of human language:

> Having mastered a language, one is able to understand an indefinite number of expressions that are new to one's experience, that bear no simple resemblance and are in no simple way analogous to the expressions that constitute one's linguistic experience: and one is able, with greater or less facility, to produce such expressions on an appropriate occasion, despite their novelty and independently of detectable stimulus configurations, and to be understood by others who share this still mysterious ability. The normal use of language

is, in this sense, a creative activity. This creative aspect of normal language use is one fundamental factor that distinguishes human language from any known system of animal communication. [Chomsky, 1972, p. 100]

Chomsky's proposed solution to the problem of finite mind/ infinite language is a system of "generative grammar," the heart of which is a relatively small number of transformational rules by which semantic and phonetic representations are mapped into one another. Vroom and Yetton's (1973) decision-tree approach is a step in the right direction of developing a set of rules for deriving the "surface structure" of leadership, but I believe that their procedure still suffers the fundamental flaw of all leadership theories—the failure to recognize the creative unboundedness of leadership acts. In case it is in doubt, I believe the set of leadership acts is of the same order of magnitude as the set of sentences in a natural language. Language is after all one of the key tools of social influence.

6. *For the most part, leadership research has limited itself to looking at social influence that is of the direct, face-to-face variety.* Perhaps this is why there has been so much emphasis on personal style. But some of the most important forms of influence are remote from the behavior being induced. When I start up my car, a buzzer and a light on the dashboard instruct me to fasten my seat belt. So I am under the impersonal influence of those devices. But more remotely, I am being influenced by the engineer who designed the devices, by the legislators and bureaucrats who required their use, and by Ralph Nader who caused us to think about auto safety in the first place. Does it make sense to think of these influences as instances of "leadership"?

One of my colleagues at the University of Illinois, Greg Oldham, is trying to broaden the concept of leadership to include any kind of control the leader has over the environment of the group member (Oldham, 1974). I feel very ambivalent about this effort. It accords with my intuition that social influence ought not to be limited to visible, face-to-face interactions. On the other hand, it so diffuses the concept of leadership that it ceases to be an identifiable phenomenon at all, and seems to merge with the whole field of "management." Nevertheless, my inclination is to go with Oldham and broaden the concept to include all of the indirect, remote, and invisible influences of leadership on behavior.

An interesting diversion is suggested by this point. Suppose leadership is a residual category to which we assign the causal responsibility for events we cannot otherwise explain. Several conclusions follow very rapidly. (1) Once the category exists we will try to fill it, so more and more things will be attributed to "leadership," especially in turbulent environments where there are a great number of unique events to make sense of. So we should expect the concept of leadership to expand in high-variety environments and to contract in low-variety environments. Does this suggest a possible study of what people in different settings mean by the term leadership? (2) Leadership results from our assigning *personal* responsibility for events, rather than from the workings of impersonal forces. This assignment is more likely after a success than after a failure. This refines the previous point, to wit, that leadership as an attributional category will expand only upon successful coping with turbulence. (3) Cultures vary in the degree to which personhood is a central concept. It is striking to walk from the Egyptian rooms into the Greek rooms of the British Museum and be hit with the shift in god-forms from animal to human characteristics. (Does this have anything to do with Greece's being the crucible of democracy?) Back from the diversion to the main point—that leadership does (should?) include very remote influences on behavior.

7. One of the least visible influences on our behavior is the language we use. "Sharing a language with other persons provides the subtlest and most powerful of all tools for controlling the behavior of these other persons to one's advantage" (Morris, 1949, p. 214). This suggests an experimental paradigm that could spawn a hundred fascinating studies: How is a leader's effectiveness related to the language overlap with his subordinates? (Is it conceivable that democratic leadership works because it promotes language-sharing? Does that mean that the comparative advantage of democratic leadership will be greatest when language overlap is initially minimal?) My guess is that it should be relatively easy to manipulate language overlap experimentally. But this forces us to ask the question, what does it mean to "share a language"?

One source of not-sharing is having a different lexicon or vocabulary, that is, different words appear in two different languages. This is the less troublesome type of not-sharing (or language-mismatch) because it carries its own signal of mismatch; it generates the question, "What does that mean?" A second and more serious type of language-mismatch is when the lexicons are identical but the "semanticons" differ, that is, when the meanings attached to the words are different. In this case the signal of mismatch is implicit in the way the words are *used*, and thus much more difficult to detect than lexical mismatches. The meaning of a word is the set of ways in which it is used (Parkinson, 1968; Wittgenstein, 1974). Note that this suggests an operational way of experimentally generating different semanticons for the leaders and their subordinates: Give each of them a different set of uses of certain key terms—a sort of word history.

This also says something about how languages come to be shared—by sharing experiences and *talking* about them, that is, by using words and thereby establishing shared meanings. But this suggests that languages evolve when a given lexicon is used to describe new events. That is, meanings change roughly as fast as the enacted environment changes, and the rate of language renewal will need to keep pace if leadership effectiveness is to be sustained. Does this suggest that one of the neglected leadership functions is language renewal? And let me stress a crucial point: It is not sufficient to enact a shared environment; it has to be talked about. Perhaps this is why several studies have shown strong relationships among the number of committees or the frequency of committee meetings and the rates of program change (e.g., Hage, Aiken, & Marrett, 1971). What is communicated in a communication is not words, but meanings.[1]

8. *In placing stress on language overlap and meaning creation, we may be missing an obvious point—that the leader's subtle use of the language may also be an important factor in determining his effectiveness, both in enhancing his credibility and in manag-*

1. See Kurt Back's (1962, pp. 35–48) distinction between a stimulus and a message.

ing the influence process. Let me give you an example. In Britain, plural verbs are used in certain places where we would use the singular tense, and this inevitably reveals something about the speaker's perception of the relation of group to individual. To be specific, one says, "The government *are* . . ." and "Leeds United *have* defeated West Ham," whereas we would use *is* and *has* and thus reveal our attitude toward the unified action of collectivities. I have no idea how to begin to measure or quantify this notion of subtlety in usage of language, but surely it must be related to the leader's empathy or sensitivity to his colleagues.

9. *What does it mean to be an "effective" leader?* My perception of research in the field is that effectiveness is typically conceptualized as "performance of the subordinate group"—usually some kind of output measure—or perhaps as compliance or adherence to the leader's directives. In any case, the effectiveness concept and measure is invariably a behavioral one. The "good" leader is one who can get his subordinates to *do* something. What happens if we force ourselves away from this marriage to behavioral concepts? What kind of insights can we get if we say that the effectiveness of a leader lies in his ability to make activity meaningful for those in his role set—not to change behavior but to give others a sense of understanding what they are doing, and especially to articulate it so they can communicate about the meaning of their behavior. Musicians use this kind of terminology to describe their reactions to conductors. Faulkner (1973) quotes musicians as saying of their conductor, "[he] gives us gestures of expression but they're not showing us his meaning," or, "He doesn't communicate with technique or with words. He sort of looks surprised when we play," or they refer to the difference between "playing notes" and "making music." Now some of these expressions refer to an internal, nonarticulated sense of understanding. But the content of the feeling cannot be communicated (except that you may be able to communicate that you have it without describing it). If in addition the leader can *put it into words,* then the meaning of what the group is doing becomes a *social* fact. That is terribly important! The meaning can be exchanged, talked about, modified, amplified, and used for internal processing of information.

The real power of Martin Luther King was not only that he had a dream, but that he could describe it, that it became public, and therefore accessible to millions of people. This dual capacity (surely it is much more than a mere trait) to make sense of things *and* to put them into language meaningful to large numbers of people gives the person who has it enormous leverage. (I must confess to racking my creative insight to the breaking point to find the right phrase to describe this capacity, but the effort was, sad to report, in vain!) One final word: This capacity to go public with sense making involves putting very profound ideas in very simple language. Perhaps that is why it is so rare. But its rarity should not dissuade us from its study.

So far in these notes, I have flirted with language concepts in several different places at two or three different levels. *At one level* I was trying to say that the word "leadership," by its existence, has influenced how we, as social scientists, see the world and how we take an undifferentiated reality and cut it up into one set of chunks rather than another set. Although the uses of a word constitute its meaning, the meaning has at least an instantaneous autonomy and control over the nature of variations in its use. Part of the aim of this conference is to overcome this semantic inertia and to accelerate variations in use of the term leadership. Which of the proposed variations are *selected* for attention by the other participants will depend on how the variations are phrased. But whether these different meanings of the term leadership are *retained* in usage will probably depend on how strong are the participants' vested interests in the current meaning. This process of changing the meaning of a word is an instance of what Wittgenstein has called a "language game." Does this language game (changing the meaning of a word) include processes that we feel comfortable thinking about as "leadership"?

At a second level, I was saying that a leader's understanding of the subtleties of meaning are important to his effectiveness. We can sharpen this point by noting that thought and communication involve a multiplicity of language games in which not only individual words have different meanings, but words in general may have different functions. In part, "understanding the subtleties" requires knowing which language game you are playing. For example, Wittgenstein identifies "reporting an event" and "giving and obeying orders" as distinct language games. The phrase "Five slabs!" in the former game means "There are five slabs," and in the latter game "Bring me five slabs." A more appropriate title for this essay would be "Leadership is a *collection of* language games."

At a third level, how linguistics (and, in particular, Chomsky) has approached the study of language provides a prototype worth imitating. I have already mentioned the creative use of language as an obvious fact that any explanation of language must deal with. No sophisticated data collection procedures and multivariate analyses are needed to establish that fact. Equally important, and I have not yet mentioned this point, is that Chomsky has done two things to make possible a formal, and therefore tractable but still insight-rich, study of language.

First, he distinguished between linguistic competence and performance. By competence he meant those aspects of speech that are person-independent and due only to the formal structure of the language. By performance, he meant how the language is actually spoken, with frequent errors of syntax, stopping and starting over, and so forth. By focusing on language competence, and ignoring issues of performance for the time being, he has been able to formulate solvable problems about the formal structure of language.

Second, by inventing the concepts of phonetic and semantic representations, he has been able to define the field of syntactics, again allowing him to formulate solvable problems, but in a way that the simplifications can be relaxed when a foothold has been established in syntactics.

There is another issue here. Chomsky is interested in understanding the human mind, as opposed to behavior, and he sees language as a way of gaining insight into mind, inasmuch as language is a creation of mind. I have not yet traced the implications of these strategies of inquiry for research on leadership, nor am I certain that they would help leadership research if applied. But they do represent an approach to inquiry that is radically different from that followed by leadership researchers. And thus, if experimented with, they represent a potential source of creative insight.

Although this essay is meant to be an informal set of notes that raises certain issues without necessarily developing them fully, it may be worthwhile to say a few more words about Wittgenstein's concept of language games before concluding. This is a difficult task inasmuch as he nowhere provides a concise definition of either language or language game—and with good reason. To be consistent with his philosophical position, he can establish the meaning of a word only by using it! Just as chess, baseball, and ring-around-the-rosie seem to share no characteristic in common, they still belong to the fuzzy-edged set of things called games. The same with language. Language is used to describe pain and other nonsharable inner sensations, to communicate, to express an idea, and so forth. These are all uses of language, but very different uses, with some overlapping characteristics between some of the uses, but no single attribute common to all. To quote Wittgenstein (1974):

> But how many different kinds of sentences are there? Say assertion, question, and command?— There are *countless* kinds, countless different kinds of use of what we call "symbols," "words," "sentences." And this multiplicity is not something fixed, given once and for all; but new types of language, new language-games, as we may say, come into existence, and others become obsolete and get forgotten. . . . Here the term "language-game" is meant to bring into prominence the fact that *speaking* of language is part of an activity, or of a form of life. . . . If you do not keep the multiplicity of language-games in view, you will perhaps be inclined to ask questions like: "What is a question?"— Is it the statement that I do not know such-and-such, or the statement that I wish the other person would tell me . . . ? Or is it the description of my mental state of uncertainty?— And is the cry, "Help!" such a description? [pp. 11–12]

This quote barely begins to give an inkling of Wittgenstein's ideas on language and language games. The significance for us is twofold. First, it suggests that we begin to think of leadership, like language, as a collection of games with *some* similarities, but no single characteristic common to all of them. Second, it begins to map out the philosophical underpinnings of the role of language and meaning in leadership and behavior. At least it has had a profound influence on my own thinking about how meanings are established and what it means to communicate.

Let me conclude with a thought and a poem.

On rereading these notes, there were times when I questioned the sanity of their author. But sanity is the result of a process of social definition. How tolerantly a social system defines sanity has a profound effect on how adaptive that system can be. Marginally sane acts are sources of creativity. Define them to be insane, rather than merely eccentric, and you rob the system of that source of creativity. The fact that this conference may define these ideas to be intriguing rather than insane says something unexpectedly healthy about the field of leadership.

This poem is from Chuang-Tsu (fourth century B.C.):

How shall I talk of the sea to the frog,
    if he has never left his pond?

How shall I talk of the frost to the bird of the summer land,
    if it has never left the land of its birth?

How shall I talk of life with the sage,
    if he is the prisoner of his doctrine?

References

Back, K. W. Can subjects be human and humans be subjects? In J. H. Criswell, H. Solomon, & P. Suppes (Eds.), *Mathematical methods in small group processes.* Stanford, Calif.: Stanford University Press, 1962.

Bateson, G. *Steps to an ecology of mind.* New York: Chandler, 1972.

Chomsky, N. *Language and mind* (Enlarged ed.). New York: Harcourt Brace Jovanovich, 1972.

Dansereau, F., Graen, G., & Haga, W. A vertical dyad linkage approach to leadership within formal organizations: A longitudinal investigation of the role making process. *Organizational Behavior and Human Performance,* 1975, **13,** 46–78.

Faulkner, R. R. Orchestra interaction: Some features of communication and authority in an artistic organization. *Sociological Quarterly,* 1973, **14,** 147–157.

Hage, J., Aiken, M., & Marrett, C. B. Organization structure and communications. *American Sociological Review,* 1971, **36,** 860–871.

Mitroff, I. I., & Pondy, L. R. On the organization of inquiry: A comparison of some radically different approaches to policy analysis. *Public Administration Review*, 1974, **34**, 471–479.

Morris, C. W. *Signs, language and behavior.* New York: Prentice-Hall, 1949.

Oldham, G. R. Some determinants and consequences of the motivational strategies used by supervisors (Doctoral dissertation, Yale University, 1974). *Dissertation Abstracts International*, 1974, **35**, 2477-B. (University Microfilms No. 74–25,750)

Parkinson, G. H. R. (Ed.). *The theory of meaning.* London: Oxford University Press, 1968.

Vroom, V. H., & Yetton, P. *Leadership and decision making.* Pittsburgh: University of Pittsburgh Press, 1973.

Wittgenstein, L. *Philosophical investigations* (G. E. M. Anscombe, Trans.). Oxford: Basil Blackwell, 1974.

Commentary

Somewhere we have lost sight of the "deep structure" or meaning of leadership. Bateson has said that our language is thing-oriented and is weak in describing relationships or processes. We seem to force ourselves into narrow conceptualizations of variegated phenomena. Pondy notes that we have traditionally documented the uniformity in leadership, getting dense coverage of too limited an area. Drawing an analogy between leadership and language, he posits that leadership research has concentrated on "surface structures": sounds, actions, and expressions that are measurable. The "deep structures," nuances, meanings, and fragile relationships, are too ethereal to be observed.

Tangible evidence of Pondy's contention was demonstrated in his workshop. When asked to define leadership, most participants responded with descriptions of certain kinds of individuals who influence others through various behaviors and traits. But when asked to recount their earliest experiences with leadership, their responses dealt with processes involving individuals whose leadership carried deep symbolic meanings rich in context and vivid memories. Leadership was seen as occurring over time, evoking strong feelings, and integrating the leader, group, and system as one.

In hammering at concepts and definitions we have reduced leadership to its phonetics. (As Humpty Dumpty says, "When I use a word, it means just what I choose it to mean, neither more nor less.") You can pick a particular leadership style or emphasize considerate or structuring behaviors. You can do this or that, and what is done is constrained to phonetics—the lyrics without the score.

As Weick argued previously, leadership is an infinite set of inputs and outputs, decisions and nondecisions, and like language, infinitely creative. Defining leadership effectiveness as the performance of the subordinate group is a suffocating fragmentation of the process.

To look at the "deep structure" of leadership, we may want to look at the leader's use of language to make activities meaningful for others. Great leaders articulate and share their dreams with others, and through this understanding make their dreams accessible. This access is to the things people care about most: meaning, good feelings, a sense of control. How leaders share themselves, and through this sharing breathe power and purpose into others, is an intriguing area for research.

In the next chapter, Vaill explores some ways to document the variety in leadership. His mercurial remarks range across the whole of social science research—from questioning eight assumptions researchers often accept, to a potpourri of hypotheses for describing high-performing systems and their leaders, to trying to understand Humpty Dumpty rather than continuing to push him down from the wall.

MML

6. *Toward a Behavioral Description of High-Performing Systems*

Peter B. Vaill

I. Preface

The first thirty-nine hypotheses, which constitute the heart of this essay, were produced in one four-hour burst following a lecture by Eric Trist. A few days later the eight assumptions and the remarks about joint optimization were written. Of the various comments that precede the list of hypotheses, the one in which I am most interested concerns the search for "laws of joint optimization."

Those who have read this study have found it interesting, but also rather frustrating and even baffling. When pressed, I have found myself unable to say what a "high-performing system" is, and I am about ready to stipulate that the question which opens the essay is at best a way of getting started and at worst is misleading and probably a red herring.

I feel I should say that the forty-seven hypotheses are "intuitive leaps" and not deductions from any theory, although some (e.g., 21) frankly take issue with prevailing theory. Some hypotheses I am in love with (e.g., 5, 12, 14, 15, 27, 28, 39, and 47), and some I am not interested in. I should also say that I am not interested at the moment in doing research to verify any of these hypotheses —at least research as conventionally conceived. I feel this way because behind the hypotheses is some kind of dimly perceived gestalt that will evaporate entirely if I become analytical too soon. The gestalt is the "it" that behaves according to the as-yet-unstated laws of joint optimization.

This may all be too mystical for you, and, if it is, that is all right. If it is not, I would like some help in figuring out what the "it" is.

II. High-performing systems

This study seeks to answer the following question: When a group of men using some collection of technologies is performing, in relation to some predefined goals or standards, in a way that may be described as "excellent" or "outstanding" or "high performing," what events may be observed in such systems?

The question contains a number of loosely defined terms that, for the moment, will be left undefined. An overly restrictive definition will prevent us from engaging in the acts of imaginative hypothesizing that are the main foci of this essay. Perhaps more clarity can be introduced, though, if it is stipulated that the focus is on systems that are "doing better" than óther similar systems composed of similar men, using similar technologies, pursuing similar goals, or adhering to similar standards.

Before going on to fashion some behavioral hypotheses about "what is happening" in such high-performing systems, several key underlying assumptions should be stated. These assumptions are offered without defense or proof.

1. The first assumption is that most of what we think we know about the performance of work systems derives from research in settings where the human members of the system are not there voluntarily. We have tended to study employees—people who have to work for a living—and we have studied employers —people in a role of stewardship relative to external stock-holders, whose basic responsibility is to make the organization work in the financial interest of these stockholders.

2. The second assumption is that most organizational research has been problem-oriented: the research has been done to throw light on the causes of unsatisfactory performance. Even where the research itself has been purely descriptive in purpose, the underlying motive for conducting or sponsoring it has tended to be normative, i.e., to learn how to make the organization work better.

3. A third assumption follows—that one can extrapolate from the causes of ineffective performance to the causes of more effective performance. For example, if opportunity for decision making is found to be lacking and an effect on performance seems to exist, then it should follow that more opportunity for decision making will produce improved performance.

4. The criteria for evaluating whether a work system is performing satisfactorily or not have tended to be comparative. If one system, for example, is not as profitable as another apparently similar system, then the first system can be assumed to be relatively less effective.

5. *Either* the human *or* the nonhuman (e.g., technological) components have tended to be the focus of most research, with major simplifying assumptions about the components-not-being-studied being made by the researcher.

6. A somewhat casually thought-out assumption has been that the system should be studied in accord with a priori specifications. The internal boundaries of the organization used by management for its control purposes have been permitted to define the system to be investigated. Specification of the system to be studied has tended not to be an empirical question.

7. A major category of research findings has been the observed discrepancy between what is supposed to be happening in the system and what is actually happening. The assumption: What is *supposed* to be happening is taken as the standard for a desirable level of system functioning.

8. At key interfaces between the system in question and entities in its environment, the assumption has been made that improved coordination and integration of interests "across the boundary" are desirable.

Much of what we think we know about management and organizational behavior seems to rest on assumptions such as these. This list of eight assumptions has usually been taken for granted in most studies. Occasionally a study calls one or two of these assumptions into question, but rarely has the whole list been questioned. (Assumption 4 has been questioned fairly frequently. Assumption 5's bankruptcy has been a major tenet of the so-called "socio-technical systems" approach to organizational research and improvement. Some academic organization theorists have fastidiously avoided Assumption 2.)

This study grows originally out of questioning Assumption 5, the "man vs. machine" assumption. The concept of "joint optimization" as it has been developed by the socio-technical systems researchers was taken seriously as an alternative assumption. However, as the phenomenon of joint optimization was considered more carefully, it became clear that all the other assumptions on the list had to be questioned as well. *It is possible that a high-performing system, as defined at the outset of this essay, cannot be fully understood so long as any of these assumptions are accepted without question.*

In the remainder of this essay, two things are done. First, the concept of "joint optimization" is discussed more fully. Then I ask: When joint optimization is occurring in a system, what is happening?

In an informal lecture[1] Eric Trist (of the Tavistock Institute of Human Relations and the University of Pennsylvania's Wharton School) spelled out what "joint optimization" means in a work system. Basically, a work system is some organized collection of men and things. The "things" may be tools and machinery, from the simplest to the most complex elements. The men may function as individuals, in twos and threes, in groupings of a dozen or so, in large organizations, or in combinations of these. To make the system work, the problem is to get the things, whose behavior is governed by one set of laws, to interface effectively with the men, whose behavior is governed by another set of laws. The laws that govern the behavior of things are physical—for instance, laws of mechanics, thermodynamics, hydraulics, and electronics. The laws that govern the behavior of men are the laws of psychology, sociology, and anthropology, as well as the laws of biology, which may be better understood. Each set of laws (one for inanimate, one for animate) has its own limits, imperatives, and opportunities. Each is discoverable and manageable by its own particular brands of scientific investigation.

1. These remarks were made at a conference on socio-technical systems, held at the Wharton School, University of Pennsylvania, November 1, 1972.

We may go on to observe, from Trist's basic premise, that history has shown man's tendency to reduce one class of laws to the other. Perhaps the strongest pressure has been to investigate and interpret the behavior of animate entities by the laws of the inanimate. Many theorists have commented on the fascination psychology has had for physics. It is not hard to demonstrate that the psychological vocabulary owes more to physics than to any other field. But the reverse process occurs as well. The history of Romanticism is, in one sense, the history of the attempt to investigate and interpret the physical world in humanistic terms.

"Joint optimization" is that stream of processes in a work system in which the various elements are behaving according to, *but not beyond,* the limits set by the laws that govern their behavior, and in which the behavior of any particular element is not preventing some other element from behaving in accordance with the laws that govern it.

A simple example: An automobile may be capable, within the laws that govern it, of going 200 mph. But a particular man may *not* be capable, within the laws that govern him, of driving it that fast. Therefore, at 200 mph, a condition of joint optimization does not exist. The system is unstable and probably cannot endure at that level of performance. Conversely, the man may be capable of controlling an automobile at 200 mph, but the particular car he is driving may not be capable of that sustained speed. Therefore, at or near 200 mph, joint optimization is again not occurring. Thus, the problem of joint optimization here would be, "What is the optimal level of performance for a particular man in a particular car under a particular set of road conditions?"

This abstract discussion can be brought to a concrete focus in the day-to-day conduct of organizations. The problem is seen when we find men doing "well-engineered" jobs that they find intolerable. And it is seen when we find "well-qualified" men doing work that does not call forth what they have to contribute. It is also seen when we find men "misusing" equipment and other resources because they must behave in ways that they prefer. In the first two cases, the man is asked to behave contrary to the laws governing *his* behavior in order that the technology may be operated in accordance with laws governing *its* behavior. In the third case, we see men behaving according to the laws of their behavior at the expense of the laws governing the technology's behavior.

The problem of joint optimization in a work system is a research issue of the greatest importance. It is no longer satisfactory to design one part of the system carefully and let the other parts fall into step. Nor is it any longer satisfactory to design the several elements of the system carefully and expect them to integrate themselves automatically.

We need some "laws of joint optimization"—some statements at a fairly high level of generality about the limits of human-operated technologies. These laws are probably not fully deducible from the laws we now know of men and the laws we now know of technologies. It is, possibly, a set of laws for a new phenomenon that we seek.

A first and tentative step is to look for real-world systems of a fairly conventional and simple kind and to see if we can state what is happening in these systems when they are working well. In the list of hypotheses that follows, I have made some use of what goes on in business organizations and other formal work systems, but I have made at least as much use of what I think goes on in settings we do not often think about as relevant to management studies. I mean athletic organizations, performing arts (such as music, theater, and dance), and various craft specialties.

In the list of hypotheses that follows, it is probably possible to group the several statements in some more organized way than I have. But I have refrained from this because I think a taxonomy is premature.

1. One may observe a great deal of experimentation and rehearsal in an HPS.[2] Various ways of operating the system are tried. There seems to be only temporary fixation (if at all) on "the one best way" to operate the system.

2. No one kind of human behavior dominates the system. There is a considerable amount of shifting around among various manual and mental activities.

---

2. HPS stands for "High-Performing System."

3. One may note members of the system paying attention to "arranging the environment" within which activity is going to occur. Things have to be "just right." Failure to achieve the right arrangement of environmental conditions is sometimes cause for system members to fail to begin the activity, or to terminate it abruptly.

4. A private language and set of symbols arise among members of the system for talking about its conduct and problems. These language systems relate to the nuances and complexities of the system's operation. These language systems are often thought by outside observers to be unintelligible jargon, and the functionality of the language is missed.

5. Members evolve a set of indices of system performance that are system-specific and that may not relate easily to any other system, even one that is superficially identical.

6. When the system is not operating satisfactorily, relative to members' system-specific performance criteria, the members become greatly agitated and upset. The consequences of "failure" often seem to observers to be greatly magnified. Observers may feel members "take things too seriously."

7. There may be a public, objective theory or "rule book" about how to do the thing that the HPS is doing, but there will always be discrepancies between this public recipe and what the HPS is actually doing. This may be called the "Doug Sanders' backswing" hypothesis.[3]

8. The initial involvement in the activity of the HPS will often have been voluntary for members and will have occurred when they were relatively young. At some point the member will have "turned pro."

9. Where there are three or more people involved in a particular HPS, a set of explicit values and ideologies about what the system does and why it does it will tend to arise.

10. Communication from members to outsiders about how and why the HPS operates as it does will tend to be in platitudes

3. Doug Sanders, the professional golfer, is known for his very short backswing when driving from the tee. During the 1960s he was one of golf's leading money winners.

and generalities, or by means of showing rather than telling. Members will feel and often say, "There's no way I can explain it to you."

11. Hours of work, intensities of effort, and other style variables will tend to be determined by the imperatives of Hypotheses 1, 2, 3, 4, 5, 6, and 8, rather than by external agencies that ostensibly "govern" the system.

12. Members will report "peak experiences" in connection with their participation in the HPS. They will "enthuse," "bubble," "communicate joy and exultation."

13. Performance breakthroughs occur in unplanned ways. Hypothesis 12 will be especially obvious on these occasions. Members will account for the event in relatively nonoperational idioms, such as "we finally got it all together."

14. The inanimate elements of the system are often anthropomorphized by members of an HPS. Machines become people. Various elements are assumed to have a psychology all their own to which a member feels he must relate. (For example, ships are always women.)

15. A member, therefore, develops a personal relationship between himself and his equipment. ("A pole is a very personal thing to a pole vaulter"—Bob Seagren.)[4]

16. Observers may come to feel that members "live, eat, sleep, and breathe" the activity. This perception on the part of observers is an important clue that members may be involved in an HPS.

17. External controls on the activity of the HPS are seen by members as at best irrelevant, and at worst as positive impediments to performance. Circumvention of the rules tends to be overt and nonapologetic (see Hypotheses 27 and 28).

18. Members may seem to possess general abilities that can be transferred to other systems. This assumption is often incor-

---

4. Seagren made this comment to Jim McKay of ABC Television while being interviewed about the supposed illegality of the pole he wanted to use at the 1972 Olympics in Munich.

rect. A .350 hitter is not just a .350 hitter, typically, but a .350 hitter in a context.

19. The system does not have a clear OFF/ON character. Members may regard it as ON when it seems OFF to observers, and OFF when it seems ON.

20. Members seek relief from the pressures of participation in the HPS according to criteria that are internal to the system—e.g., its current phase of operations and the needs and expectations of other members. External schedules for relief and breaks are usually regarded by members as inappropriate.

21. In HPSs, the activities involved in task performance and the activities involved in fellowship and the maintenance of social solidarity within the system may be the same activities to a much greater extent than in non-HPSs.

22. Leaders in HPSs will tend to be persons who are perceived by members as experts in the techniques of the system's basic activity. A leader's initial status, influence, credibility, and prestige will derive from the demonstration of expertise.

23. Leaders of HPSs will not be "generalists," i.e., perceived by members as no longer fully expert in performing the system's basic activities.

24. The process of leadership in an HPS will tend to be by example and precept. Leaders will be perceived by members as "pacesetters."

25. Members of HPSs will exhibit a consciousness of the history, tradition, and lore of the system's activity and perhaps of the particular system itself (e.g., "putting on the Yankee pinstripes"). Members' consciousness of the system's lore may persist long after a particular system has ceased to be an HPS.

26. Where there are many systems performing a similar set of activities, a "hall of fame" phenomenon will arise. Membership in the hall of fame will tend to be associated with membership in an HPS.

27. The social value of the output of an HPS is problematic. Entities in the HPSs' environment will not automatically be "pleased" with its output.

28. Efforts on the part of entities in the HPSs' environment to call forth a particular kind and quality of output will tend to depress motivation in the HPS unless the function described in Hypothesis 29 is performed with extraordinary care and effectiveness.

29. HPSs will tend to evolve various boundary roles for mediating their relations with the environment: managers, handlers, advance men, press agents, etc.

30. Members of HPSs will tend to discover potentialities in their technology and their separate talents that are not predictable by observers, or deducible by examining the characteristics of various elements taken singly.

31. Members will be found adding to and elaborating upon the inanimate objects of an HPS. They will invent a variety of jigs, props, fixtures, and signalling devices that function to improve their relation to the inanimate objects—make the inanimate objects work better or last longer.

32. Members tend to engage in a wide range of maintenance activities on themselves and on the inanimate elements of the system. Maintenance is co-mingled with performance and is not experienced by members as a necessarily separate function.

33. Performances may be called forth from the inanimate side of an HPS that may seem to observers to be impossible. Physical laws may seem to be broken. Such is not the case, but rather the true constraints of physical laws are misperceived by observers, owing to Hypothesis 34.

34. Unless an observer is a trained performer, he cannot detect all the actions that go into the operation of the system, and often he cannot detect any but the most overt and prominent actions.

35. Some observers will be fascinated by the hidden character of system actions and will evolve research techniques (e.g., videotape instant replay) for investigating the system's operation more closely. HPSs in particular will excite such curiosity. Some observers will become knowledgeable "buffs" in regard

to the HPSs' action and may come to play critical boundary roles with respect to the system's wider environment.

36. Members may tend to develop scenarios of desirable states for the HPS to be in. A considerable amount of apparently meaningless behavior can be explained as attempts to realize these scenarios. The function of all such attempts is to prepare members to participate in the system's operation and to sustain them through its difficult moments.

37. In terms of McLuhan's (1964) hypothesis that some technologies are "hot" in the sense that their effect on a person requires little physical/psychological participation by him, members of HPSs will tend to experience the technologies of their systems as relatively "cool," i.e., that the meaning of the activity is in the doing of it.

38. Members of an HPS may tend to have a powerful aesthetic experience regarding the inanimate objects of the system and/or the system's operation. As this process unfolds for members, they may acquire aesthetic *motivation* with respect to the system and seek the experience rather than merely receive it.

39. Hypothesis 38 may be broadened to suggest that certain kinds of motivation which are not detectable in other settings may be found in HPSs. To the extent that members find participation in the HPS thrilling, they may become "thrill seekers." Activity in the HPS may provide a wide variety of sensual, affective, and cognitive experiences that, over time, members may become "motivated" to attain and re-experience. For the most part, these kinds of motivation may be relatively incomprehensible to observers. They may come to regard members so motivated as "weirdos" or "mystics."

40. When an HPS ceases to perform to its former degree of effectiveness, members will go through various stages of feeling and behavior in reaction to the decline. One such stage will be the phenomenon of "pressing."

41. When a person has been the leader of an HPS for an extended period, he will become a quasi-mythical figure, embodying

in his person much of the meaning that the work of the HPS possesses for members and afficionados.

42. Processes of attention in system members will have some attributes that are absent or dormant in non-HPSs.

43. The sense of the passage of time will correlate with the perceived temporal process of system performances and will not be a set of awarenesses apart from system operation. In short, boredom and anticipatory anxiety will tend to be absent.

44. The meaning to a member of his own and other members' behavior will be a function of system activities rather than a function of "personal values" or the norms of the wider culture.

45. Many behaviors will be automatic to the degree that a member cannot account later for how or why he did them.

46. Marvin Weisbord[5] has suggested that in HPSs people keep track of their performance in ways that may be internal and very personal, i.e., involving a highly personalized coding system that may have little meaning to anyone else.

47. HPSs exhibit a rhythm of operation that is both subjectively felt by members and objectively evident to observers. An argot will exist for describing this rhythm, for example, "tempo" (chess), "footing" (yacht racing), "wailing" (improvisational jazz), "getting it on" and "grooving"—and note that "grooving" has been extended in its application to many other activities—"taking it to . . . (the opposing team)," "traction" (term coined by W. Baldamus, 1951, pp. 45–47, to account for the tendency of an assembly line job to pull the worker along), "hitting one's stride," "having a hot hand" (basketball), and "mounting a charge" (golf). The general phenomenon to which these terms refer is that the same or improved effects are produced with substantially less effort than before the particular rhythm was achieved.

Why speculate at such length about what is going on inside what I have called a "high-performing system"? The basic answer

5. Weisbord is a well-known management consultant who made this point in conversation with the author at Bethel, Maine, in July 1974.

is that if basic systems can be better understood, the problem of improving the performance of human organizations may be eased. As noted in the list of assumptions with which this discussion began, social scientists and managers are presently groping toward improved performance levels without having in mind any norms of what is really possible. It is possible that at least some of these hypothesized properties of HPSs may provide such norms—targets, as it were—to shoot at.

It is a sobering exercise to go over the list of forty-seven hypotheses stated above and ask, in connection with each one: To what extent are we inadvertently managing our organizations today in a way that prevents the emergence of the particular condition to which the hypothesis refers? We espouse a philosophy of high performance. Our management and leadership literature is full of it. But do we *manage* and *lead* in such a way as to achieve the hypothesized conditions?

III. Presentation

I want to briefly discuss what you might call the background of Sections I and II, that is, the books I have been reading and the concerns I have been developing in recent years that led to my focus on "high-performing systems" and to the long list of hypotheses about these systems.

The first point I want to underscore is mentioned in the preface: I am not sure where to go from here with these ideas. Relative to my own professional concerns, this is a "new Gestalt" for me, and I am leery about becoming overly systematic about it too soon. I have had to struggle a bit against an orthodox urge to convert some of these hypotheses into testable propositions, create a research design, get myself a grant, and begin collecting data systematically on these things called "high-performing systems."

What I think the proper strategy should be is to keep musing on the broad issue—what is this "it" I have called a "high-performing system"? Another way to say it, which brings this essay directly within the scope of the conference, is to ask, "What is the nature of the thing the leader is leading or the manager is managing?" The eight assumptions with which I began reflect my conviction that in certain profound ways our research so far on this question has been distorted seriously by some unexamined premises. Those eight assumptions are my prime candidates. I think they have led us to conduct research in particular ways, and interpret our findings in particular ways, that may lead us *away* from understanding the thing the leader is leading, or the manager is managing.

In terms of my own professional development, I have been concerned about finding better ways of thinking about organizations for a long time. As an MBA student at the Harvard Business School, my repeated intensive exposure to case situations was a highly effective means of showing me the complexity of organizations and the capacity of organizational phenomena to transcend all attempts to capture them neatly in theories and models. I became more and more curious as I realized that you have a profound problem when you juxtapose the imperatives of action with our lack of knowledge of what it is the action-taker is acting in, i.e., this thing loosely called an "organization."

As a result, I have, fortunately, never been at all smug about my own professional acumen. My friends have heard me say many times that I am not at all sure what it is I am a professor *of.*

Let me talk for a few minutes, though, about some ideas that I think hold promise for making progress on my dilemma—and from a normative point of view, of course, I am saying it is not just my dilemma, but everyone's who would "profess" on what it is the leader is leading or the manager is managing.

First, I want to discuss my most recent excitements, for they have occurred at this conference. Karl Weick's notion of the leader's being a kind of two-way medium between external and internal phenomena is, for me, an absolutely new idea. Coupled with Jeff Pfeffer's suggestion that we need to pay more attention to the phenomenology of the leader, the outcome is a view of organizational reality that is different from what you find in most of our literature. Maybe we have to make the "it," the thing the leader is leading and the manager is managing, much more contingent on the perceptions of the action-taker than we have up until now. Maybe we have to be much more careful about what we say organizations are like, independent of the action-taker's point of view. Or put another way, we can say all we want about what organizations are like, but if we ignore the action-taker's frame of reference, we may well end up with "findings" that are irrelevant to him. (I could digress at length here on my own experience as a dean–action-taker in an academic organization, but I will spare you that and say simply instead, "Yes, when you get into the action role, you find that most of what behavioral scientists have said about organizations has very limited application.")

Karl and Jeff have reminded me of the great amount of time I spent as a graduate student studying general semantics. Those ideas helped me educate myself in the tricks we play on ourselves with words. Action-takers play tricks on themselves, but so do social scientists who presume to study the situations in which action-takers are found. There is, as a result, compounded distortion. The leader cannot talk very well about what he or she is up against, and the social scientist cannot talk very well about the leader's verbal inability. Much of the paraphernalia we have developed for studying situations—questionnaires, interview protocols, observational indices, criterion variables—rest on the assumption that the data are coherent and that our job is to invent research instruments for capturing that coherence. Perhaps the original data are not so coherent. If you interview me about how *I* delegate authority, or plan my time, or manage by objectives, I advise you to go very slowly in inducing any general propositions from my account. My capacity, and I think the capacity of most action-takers, is rather limited.

The only methodology I have ever run across that seeks actively to avoid this kind of distortion is Carl Rogers' "client-centered" interviewing method (Rogers, 1951). He developed it for another purpose, but it works as a research strategy as well as a therapeutic strategy. The data you get are not very elegant. They cannot be arrayed in a 2 × 2 matrix. They are hard to correlate with anything. But the data you obtain by that method do produce understanding of an important kind in you-the-researcher. I think understanding is what the whole business is all about.

Another vector, which I have been reminded of at this conference, is "ethnomethodology" as embodied in the work of Harold Garfinkel (1967). He is interested in the problem of how it is that we behave credibly in each other's eyes. How is it that I can produce an ongoing stream of behavior that makes sense to you, that does not seem weird to you, that does not cause you to stop me every thirty seconds to ask me what I mean or why I am doing what I am doing? In Weick's language, how is it that I can act as a medium in some kind of concert with your action as a medium so that we can "communicate," so that we can engage in an on-going exchange of messages and meanings that seems rational to us both?

Leaders have problems with credibility, and I think Garfinkel's approach is very promising for understanding those problems. To lead is to test one's credibility in the eyes of the other. By definition, there is a constant flirtation with irrationality, if you will, by the leader. The risk is to be told that some initiative seems irrational or silly to the followers. And yet, for the leader not to be testing these limits is to forgo literally the role of leader.

Another part of Garfinkel's work, which I think is very important to the study of leadership, is his emphasis on the "taken-for-granted" aspects of behavior, the processes and events that are essentially undiscussable by participants in some social interaction. He quotes conversations between people that, when transcribed on paper, are "incoherent" in a word-for-word sense. You literally cannot figure out what the parties are talking about, although they seem to be making perfect sense to each other. In order to understand them, you have to know a great deal about their prior relationship and about the context of their conversation. There is a code that has to be known in order to understand them. I think many of our research findings about human behavior derive from data that have not been "decoded." McGregor's (1960) "Theory X assumptions," for example, are not decoded. I mean that he transformed some words he heard coming out of managers' mouths into a theory about their values and, more importantly, about their behavior. The theory is persuasively presented and sounds very plausible, i.e., it describes all the trouble a manager who makes Theory X assumptions can get into.

The problem is that when you indict Theory X assumptions independently of their context, you are left unable to account for all the examples of successful leadership and management as practiced by men and women who hold the assumptions that McGregor says get you into trouble. In every executive seminar where I talk about McGregor, someone always says, "Yeah, but what about Vince Lombardi? What about General Patton? What about Attila the Hun?" et cetera. My experience has been that I am never able to deal with questions very well unless I am willing to substantially revise McGregor.

To understand a human system, and particularly a high-performing human system, I think we need richer and more vivid accounts of how the system is actually operating than orthodox social science procedures ordinarily produce. That is why my favorite sources of data are magazines such as the *New Yorker* and some of my favorite writers are people such as H. L. Mencken and Norman Mailer. Vivid narrative in which the writer's value system is not disguised holds out more promise, to me, for understanding a high-performing system, at this point in time at least, than any controlled experiment with independent and dependent variables.

Mailer's book *Of a Fire on the Moon* (1971), for example, tells as much of a technical nature about the Apollo 11 moon flight as you could ever want to know. But unlike a more "objective" account, the book also explores the *meaning* to Mailer of the facts and events. The meaning and the report are woven together; you cannot come away from the book saying, "These are the findings, and these are Mailer's conclusions from the findings." The two are intertwined in a natural and, to me, beautiful way. If you believe Ian Mitroff, this is characteristic of *all* science; but over the centuries, orthodox science has obfuscated the question by pretending to separate the results of the investigation from the values of the investigator.

I do not think you can study what I am calling a high-performing system by separating facts and values. The reason is that no two people can agree on what a high-performing system *is*. Or rather, I should say they will have trouble agreeing on an exact, operational definition of a high-performing system that can then be deductively applied to real world systems. You and I can agree that a Bach fugue is beautiful and a supreme achievement, but I am not optimistic that we will be able to agree on *why* it is; and I am almost certain that we will be unable to agree on a protocol for the composition of beautiful fugues. (Such protocols exist, of course, and you can earn college credit for memorizing them, but I assert that such protocols are basically political compromises.)

A simpler way of saying what I mean is to suggest that the intensive study of individual cases, something Abraham Maslow urged, is a promising alternative research strategy to what most of American social science has pursued—the search for general propositions that cut across individual cases. "Science" need not be identical with "general laws."

For example, my favorite High-Performing System of 1974 was the University of Southern California football team's performance against Notre Dame on November 30. With one minute to go before halftime, USC was behind 24–0. In the next 17 minutes of playing time, USC (1) scored on a pass, (2) ran back the second half kickoff 100 yards, (3) scored on a six-yard run, (4) scored on a four-yard run, (5) scored on an 18-yard pass, (6) scored on a 44-yard pass, (7) scored on a 16-yard pass, and (8) scored on a 58-yard runback of an interception. Three minutes into the fourth quarter, the score was USC 55—Notre Dame 24, and that was the final score.

It is my conviction that such an outburst of effectiveness (and such a collapse on Notre Dame's part) cannot be accounted for with a list of research-based "key factors" as derived from some comparative study of football team effectiveness. It is the *mix* and *reinforcing quality* of the variables in the situation that must be understood. There obviously was a synergy operating that can only be understood by studying the situation in all its richness and complexity. I will put my money on an investigator on the sidelines who is *open* to that richness over an investigator who is trying to validate a theory about the critical dimensions of leadership that he brought to the situation from somewhere else.

I have been saying to my colleagues and students for the past couple of years that "management is a performing art," a process to be thought of as a fluid, ongoing, unfolding thing, rather than as a set of steps, or an additive list of skills and abilities. I have advocated that we study management and leadership as performing arts, and that we teach them as performing arts. I will grant that when teaching a performing art, you may want to break down the performance into elements and have the learner practice those elements in isolation. But when you are teaching or studying a performing art, you never delude yourself that having mastered the practice of the parts, you have mastered the practice of the whole. Yet that is what I think we tend to do in the way we investigate leadership behavior; and that is why I think with those investigative methods, we are never going to understand what I am calling a High-Performing System.

The hypotheses of this discussion are, unfortunately, a list. Some of the hypotheses overlap; some may even seem to contradict one another. They are only a list, however, because they did not occur to me all at once as I mused on high-performing systems that I think I have known. My attention was on wholes, but I had to put down my ideas as parts.

I do a class demonstration from time to time on how analytic science tends to break wholes into pieces, and then cannot get the pieces back together. As I begin to talk, I pull a Johnson & Johnson cotton ball out of my pocket and begin, absentmindedly, to pull it apart. To the class it appears I am merely fidgeting. I finish my comments just as I complete the destruction of the cotton ball. Then I say, "Once having broken a social phenomenon into its constituent parts, it doesn't go back together any more easily than I can recreate my cotton ball by squeezing all these bits of fluff together."

I do not think we know what *leadership* is and what role it plays in bringing about high levels of human performance because we have approached the question as a process of "pulling apart." It is the holistic process of leadership that we need to understand. Those words I quote in one of the later hypotheses that refer to the holistically experienced rhythm of the system are very important. What those words say to me is that people *feel* something about the way the system is operating. The social scientist comes along and says, "Let me devise a research procedure to identify what that 'something' is because it is obviously very important to these people." So the procedure is devised and implemented, and one more sterile research finding goes on the shelf. Karl Weick's reference to the Mexican sierra is a perfect example of having to kill something in order to study it.

What people feel is not as important, for understanding the system, as is the fact that they are feeling it together. That is the thing to be understood—how it is that there can be a common mapping of an experience so that nothing needs to be said. The participants just know in a deep way what is happening. To ask what precisely is being felt is probably one of Ian Mitroff's Type III errors.

These general background concerns led me to the eight assumptions listed at the beginning of this discussion. To the extent that those assumptions have guided our research and theorizing, we may have been misleading ourselves. I want to close my remarks, therefore, with some further commentary on those eight assumptions.

The first assumption has to do with the nonvoluntary presence in the system of the people whose behavior we have studied. This one is not as important, perhaps, in situations where the system members have deliberately chosen the career we see them practicing and have a number of options as to which particular organization they work for. More and more studies are being done where this is the case. But the main data base for most of our basic research findings has come from nonvoluntary situations. With such starting conditions I do not see how we can expect to find inspired leadership and high levels of system performance.

The second and third assumptions have to do with why we study human behavior in organizations. When the attention of the investigator is on problem finding and problem solving, I wonder how much of the richness of the system *as it is* may be missed. It must be clear from all my hypotheses about HPSs that it is this richness of detail that has to be understood. I have said on many occasions that the study of the unintended consequences of leaders' actions will not reveal data on their capacity to produce intended consequences—something that is widely evident in human affairs, but which is grossly under-researched. The seventh assumption also gets at the motives of the investigator. Garfinkel (1967) calls the process of looking for discrepancies between "is" and "ought" a process of "collecting ironies." His point is that the discrepancy will always be there because of the difference in perspectives between the insider and the outsider. If the outsider becomes entranced with the discrepancy, however, he will miss the richness of the system as the members are experiencing it. I like to say that one's "findings" will always correlate with one's "lookings." If you ask the wrong question, you will probably get the wrong answer.

The fifth, sixth, and eighth assumptions are all matters that current organization theory is paying more and more attention to. Nevertheless, what we think we *know* about organizations tends to rest on research that has accepted these assumptions uncritically. I first began to seriously question the fifth assumption as I became familiar with "sociotechnical systems" theory and research. It is the *interplay* of social and technical phenomena which that school of thought asserts is the thing to be understood. However, most researchers do not take the time to investigate that interplay at any kind of a deep level. Instead, the social researchers get a quick spiel from the plant manager or foreman about what it is the organization does, and then they move on quickly to what it is they are really interested in—all the behavioral factors in the situation. Engineering and operations researchers do just the reverse: they treat behavior at a high level of abstraction, and technical variables at a low level of abstraction.

This situation is changing, of course, but bear in mind that I am talking about our existing knowledge base, not about our theoretical leading edges. Our existing knowledge base is heavily affected by splitting of behavioral and technical variables. Clearly, my hypotheses about HPSs try to get at the interplay, for that is one of the major keys to understanding. I also call your attention to my comments in the HPS discussion about the "laws of joint optimization," for I am talking there about the same issues.

The sixth assumption is a particularly interesting one to me. The researcher walks into the organization and announces that he or she would like to study, say, "productivity norms." Some member says that in Department X there should be plenty to see. So the researcher goes into Department X and studies productivity, comes away with some findings, writes them up as a contribution to the literature on social control and, perhaps, leadership—*and never stops to ask about the reality of Department X to the members who were found there.* Of course, the problem of determining what the system is in the first place has been a matter of theoretical concern in our field. But I suggest again that our knowledge base about organizational behavior derives heavily from studies where the problematic nature of the system in the first place was not rigorously addressed. Unless one is quite careful on this matter, I do not think it is going to be possible to find, or account for, events in which I am calling a high-performing system.

Of my eight assumptions, I think that the second and fifth can give you the most trouble when trying to study a high-performing system and the leadership behavior that is occurring within it. I have already said all I want to say about the fifth assumption, but a few more remarks on the second will be a fitting way to close.

In the applied social sciences, especially as they have been practiced in professional schools, the problem-finding/problem-solving orientation is deeply entrenched. In part this was a reaction to the purely academic orientation of theorists and researchers who were not trying to make their work relevant to managers and leaders. I have come to feel, however, that we need to readopt this "disinterested" stance of the academic theorist/researcher. A slightly different twist should be put on it, though, for the purpose of studying high-performing systems.

I want to encourage you to study situations that fascinate you *personally*. I want to suggest that you re-examine your criteria for what to study: Your access to a system is always a big factor; so is the existence of prior research; availability of funding certainly has influenced what investigators study; I am sure our academic promotion criteria also exert pressure to study certain kinds of situations and ignore others. But I want to stress the importance of your own, perhaps non-logical, fascination with a particular type of system. I want to get your values *into* the investigation rather than screen them out. I want to see more research that derives from "labors of love" rather than duty. I realize that such a deliberate stacking of the deck on the side of commitment rather than detachment raises a variety of serious questions about the validity and reliability of the learnings that you-the-investigator carry away from your studies.

But all of my own musings on the nature of high-performing systems lead me to the conclusion that our own values have to be part of the investigation. This is so because there is no fixed definition of what shall constitute "excellence" or "high performance." A high-performing system will always be such for *someone*, someone whose values make him or her sensitive to and intrigued with all the nuances and complexities I have mentioned in my forty-seven hypotheses. In the long run, I think, this alternative strategy holds out as much promise as the more orthodox search for detached "truth."

References

Baldamus, W. *Efficiency and effort.* London: Tavistock, 1951.
Garfinkel, H. *Studies in ethnomethodology.* Englewood Cliffs, N.J.: Prentice-Hall, 1967.
Mailer, N. *Of a fire on the moon.* New York: Signet, 1971.
McGregor, D. *The human side of enterprise.* New York: McGraw-Hill, 1960.
McLuhan, H. M. *Understanding media: The extensions of man.* New York: Signet, 1964.
Rogers, C. *Client-centered therapy.* New York: Houghton Mifflin, 1951.

Commentary

Of technology and human beings. Of the inanimate and the animate. To make systems work, the things that are governed by one set of laws have to interface with the people who are governed by another set of laws. When they interface effectively, joint optimization occurs. The various elements of the system are behaving at the limits of their capabilities.

But how are they behaving? What might this interface look like? Vaill gave this abstract framework some parameters by presenting forty-seven hypotheses about how high-performing systems work. One cannot take a malfunctioning part of a system (i.e., poor communication) and expect that a replacement (better communication) will automatically lead to effectiveness and satisfaction. Neither can one assume that a part of a system, a department or a process, a skill or a technology represents the whole.

To understand a high-performing system, it is necessary not to chop it up empirically but to get inside and understand what is going on. Knowing how the system operates would help us understand the role and impact of leaders within it.

Some systems, hospitals and open schools, for example, look chaotic to observers but not to members. If we do not understand the technological as well as the human processes at the same level of abstraction as the members do, our research is not viable. What we study is usually not an empirical question (management says, "Why don't you look at the accounting department?"), which also raises the possibility that the activity may not have any intense reality for its members.

The eight assumptions that Vaill castigates are double-edged. By not understanding the system we are researching, we may miss its reality as the members see it, or we may attribute intensity of feeling to them when none is there. Finally, it is likely that we cannot tell which is which.

In the next chapter, Mitroff extends Vaill's argument by noting that the social sciences have attempted to use the methods of the physical sciences to explain human systems. Charging, as do the others, that well-structured methodologies do not work for the dilemmas of the real world, he presents a dialectical model for dealing with ill-structured problems.

MML

7. Systemic Problem Solving

Ian I. Mitroff

I feel that the social sciences are in great need of revolution. It is not that the methodology is all bad; it is just incomplete. We have been following a brand of *physical* science that never really existed.

I have been studying the social psychology of science—the personalities of scientists and their methods. The way science really works is very different from the myths about it. There was a brilliant article in *Science* (1973) called "Newton and the Fudge Factor." The author, Richard Westfall, a good historian of science, provides a strong case that Newton blatantly fudged data because the data were not sufficient at that time to warrant his conclusions.

Science is objective, but not in the simpleminded sense of excluding subjectivity. The cases of Newton and many others tell us that the traditional view of science is a fairy tale. Science would not have progressed if it followed the mythical path of logic, rationality, and objectivity. You really have to take some of the most troublesome aspects of human behavior into account, not just exclude them, in order to understand scientific discovery.

Supposedly one of the cardinal rules of science is that one should never fudge. What then do you do when you read Arthur Koestler's *The Sleep Walkers* (1959)? The foundations of modern science were created by men who were blinded by a vision, their own vision. When I did my study of the Apollo moon scientists (Mitroff, 1974), I found them to be intensely committed—so committed that they used psychological devices to reject evidence that went against their pet hypotheses. Such findings shake our myth of science.

I recently read *Zen and the Art of Motorcycle Maintenance* (Pirsig, 1974). I was impressed when the author talked about the trip into the high country, not just the high country of geography, but the cathedral of reason, the mind. In my own work I try to bridge the gap between the qualitative and the quantitative. I have very little use for worn out dichotomies such as the distinction between "hard" and "soft" sciences. I like to collect both qualitative, unstructured data and structured, quantified data. But neither of these things has much meaning to me because, except in relationship to one another, each is incomplete.

I am interested in the theory of managerial problem solving. I shall talk about what leadership has to do with that a little later. But I think that we need a broader theory of managerial problem solving before we talk about leadership. After all, when I say leadership, what do I mean? Leadership in relation to what, for what? Leadership for the sake of leadership does not make much sense to me.

The bases of a problem-solving model

What I am trying to do is build a system that will help a person get to his or her assumptions about the world—not so much for problem solving, but for problem forming. In our executive MBA program at the University of Pittsburgh, we have trained executives to go through a dialectical exercise to design the best plan for doing something, as well as to design the best counterplan against doing that something. In effect, you plan both ways before you go off and do something.

The general concept that I am working on is something I call "error of the third kind." In elementary statistics, everyone learns about Type I and Type II errors—the probability of falsely accepting or rejecting an hypothesis. The error of the third kind is much more fundamental, and we do not teach it in management schools.

The error of the third kind is the probability of solving the "wrong" problem when you should have solved the "right" problem. It is a fundamental kind of madness to solve the wrong problem precisely, and I am afraid we proliferate Type III errors in our teaching. Type III error thinking goes on when you stay within a single paradigm. To get away from the Type III error you have to examine how a problem changes as you vary the paradigm for conceptualizing it. All you can get is a relative comparison, but that has power if you begin to systematically confront some of your most cherished assumptions about a problem.

I see an emerging notion of managerial (and social science) rationality. We need new methods for solving what I call ill-structured problems. Most of the methodology that we have is for working on well-structured problems, but all the fundamental problems we have been talking about these last few days are ill-structured. The problems of ethics, field research, abortion, pollution, questions about our professions—they are all ill-structured problems. They are not consensual; we are not going to get agreement on them.

All the old methodologies of science are founded upon a strong rule of consensus, which is even mathematically incorporated through the correlation coefficient. Something is well validated. It is reliable. Jeff Pfeffer told us about all the research that has gone on with leadership, and how we do not get a lot of significant correlations. But leadership is an ill-structured concept, and we are trying to put a consensus methodology on it.

Instead, we should try to get at the different notions of leadership and perhaps develop some concepts. The well-structured statements may follow later. (By the way, it is not an either-or situation because for every well-structured system, there are ill-structured aspects. For every ill-structured system, there are well-structured aspects, or else we could not even begin a discussion.) Most of our methodology in the social and physical sciences is for well-structured problems, problems in which the data are clear. Ackoff (1974) has a good way of putting it. He calls well-structured problems "exercises" because they are preformulated, predigested problems found mostly at the end of textbooks. Engineering is a prime example because most of the textbook problems are so well defined. You know when you get to an answer, and you know when you are screwing up.

Real problems do not possess any of those characteristics. They are fuzzy; they can be formulated more than one way; the variables are all mixed together. Ackoff says that "Nature is not organized in the same way as universities are." Because a university puts physics here and psychology over there in some other building does not mean that the real world does. The real world does not make those kinds of distinctions. It is only narrow people who have been trained in narrow ways who perform this bifurcation; real problems are all mixed up.

When we ran the course for executives in Pittsburgh, we had no textbook problems. Each participant was a manager—many were presidents of their own companies. We told them, "You're all facing real problems. We want you to bring them in, and we'll see if we can help you formulate your problem in umpteen different ways to help you avoid making a Type III error." This also meant that we as instructors had to be prepared to learn, and that was a challenge. We had to talk about real problems and how to conceptualize them in different ways.

The first element of the problem-solving model is the error of the third kind. The second element is a dialectic.

A graduate student and I have written a little computer program to help train managers to think dialectically about real problems. We tried writing something that would be fun. In one exercise, a person would sit down in front of a console and play "Beat the Computer." He would listen to two experts tell him how to play a game of uncertainty. If the player picked a certain row, he did not know what column the computer would pick, but he received whatever money or points there were at the intersection of the column and row. Those of you who know something about game theory know that there is no one unambiguous, unequivocal rule telling how to optimize your return. There are several rules, so it is a natural situation for a dialectic.

The person sits down and hears two experts fight. One expert is called Smiley, and the other expert is called Grumpy. Smiley plays the maxi-max or optimistic game strategy. Grumpy plays the pessimistic or mini-max game strategy. The question is, how do people learn in a situation when they are confronted with conflicting experts? Players have the chance to listen to structured disagreement between people who lay out their world views. The question becomes one of how the subjects behave.

There was a second part of the exercise called "Freud" that analyzed the subject's views toward problem solving. It found out how the person felt about dialectical thinking. (We called it two-way thinking because most people are not familiar with the term dialectical. No use turning off people with terms that are not crucial.) To think dialectically, the player had to be prepared to admit that both P and not P or Plan A and its extreme opposite, Not Plan A, make sense simultaneously.

This interrogation procedure, or dialectical approach, helps players strategically plan what the generic label of the problem is. Problems decay over time; they never stay static. Trivial problems are the ones that stay static. Textbook exercises are bad because they are solved once and for all. Real problems are never solved once and for all. In the 1930s and '40s the unemployment problem may have been solved by keeping it within bounds, but it always comes up again.

Myths, too, have their lifetime function, their lifetime survival function. The myths that probably survive the longest—like the great archetypal stories of cultures—are the ones that pull upon and play to deep psychological needs that never will be extinguished. The notion of mythic information is very different from the use of scientific information. Mythic information is purposely redundant because a good story never suffers in the retelling. Everything that traditional scientific information sees as a negative, myth incorporates as a positive.

Myths are like poetry. They explain human nature in terms of contradictions. You cannot explain human nature in terms of consistency. There are logicians working today on systems of logic that throw out the law of contradiction, suggesting that something cannot be both P and Not P at the same time. In real life, there are times to say, "I like him but I don't like him. I hate him and I love him." We are completely torn by contradiction. We have to come up with a system of logic to capture that complexity.

The third element of my problem-solving model is the systems concept. When I say something is a systems model, I am making two basic assertions: One, the parts do not have any existence independent of other parts. That is the ontological premise—that the parts of a thing do not exist in isolation from one another. You can break them apart. Conceptually, reductionist thinkers like to do that, but what they are actually doing is ignoring the connections. It is not that the connections do not exist; thinkers are just not studying them, and hence they are committing the Type III errors that come from working only on one part.

The second assertion is epistemological. This says, "I can't really understand the behavior of the parts independently of the whole. I can achieve a certain kind of understanding, but I can't achieve a true understanding."

The systems approach also says that systems have no absolute beginning or ending points of inquiry. That is why the APA journal format is so silly. It gives the impression of a natural stopping or ending point. Any real inquiry terminates not with an answer but with a question.

Leadership, the management of large-scale, ill-structured problems, has no absolute starting or ending point—so the whole reductionist line is silly.

These three elements—errors of the third kind, dialectical thinking, and the systems approach—form the basis for the problem-solving model.

A model of systemic problem solving

When I present my model, Step One is simply a convenient place to begin, not the true point of beginning. The first step is the felt existence of a problematic situation, which does not mean the identification of the well-defined problem as you will find it in APA journals. The problem with most problems is to find what the problem really is. That is what real problem solving is all about. To avoid a Type III error, you must examine a number of formulations of the problem before you can be sure of solving the right one. Some people want to call the problematic situation "reality." I do not like that term, because reality is really a function of the whole model—it is not located in one little box.

The problem of the Type III error is the problem of gaining representation of the system. That is something not taught. It is inconceivable in most schools. We hand out all the paradigms and preselected puzzles—"*This* is a linear programming problem," "*This* is a dynamic programming problem," or even worse, "*This* is an S-R problem," or "*This* is a contingency problem." These paradigms are all terribly seductive because you can explain the whole world with them, or at least try to, but a terrible amount is lost in the translation, to put it mildly.

So, the first step of problem solving is what I call the act or art of conceptualization—going from the felt existence of a problem, invoking some conceptualization, to a conceptual model. A conceptual model is not the same as a scientific model that assumes hard-nosed experimentation and conclusive results. Experiments are not conclusive and irrefutable. A great fuzziness and a whole host of assumptions underlie every experiment. There is a lot of talk in contemporary philosophy of science about the Duhem (1914/1962) thesis: *All* experiments are inconclusive. This does not mean that you cannot conclude things from experiments,

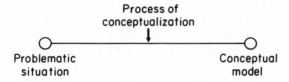

Figure 1. The conceptualizing phase.

but the experiments are never as tight, rigid, and conclusive as Type I–Type II error thinkers seem to believe.

The first step of the model is conceptual and dialectical. There is no absolute assurance of minimizing a Type III error, but the best we can do in a qualitative sense is examine the most radically distinct conceptualizations of the problem. The only way you do good scientific research is by examining *all* the different conceptualizations of the problem. In Jungian terms, this is where intuitive thinking and intuitive feeling come in. Intuition is the function that spells out possibilities. It is not concerned with developing things in detail; rather it is concerned with giving broad pictures.

Let me give you an example. A manager of a large office building was experiencing many complaints about the poor service of the elevators in the building. When the complaints reached the point where he could not ignore them any longer, he called in a team of consulting engineers. You know what the consulting engi-

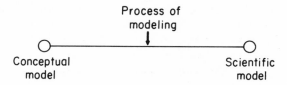

Figure 2. *The modeling phase.*

neers are going to recommend—an engineering solution to the problem: more elevators, speeding up the elevators—technological, fix-it-up types of solutions. These solutions turned out to be prohibitively expensive. Fortunately, the manager in this case asked a psychologist to make a recommendation. His solution was much cheaper. He located the problem in *people* and the stress of waiting. By installing mirrors in the lobby, he played upon the vanity of the people because they liked to look at themselves. By conceptualizing the problem in a different way, he cheaply and efficiently solved it by speeding up the perception of the passage of time, rather than by technologically speeding up the elevators.

The next step of the model we might call "modeling" because its purpose is to come to the scientific model. Once you have selected a conceptual model of the problem, you want to confine it. You want to make it highly structured so you can deduce some important conclusions to take action on.

The next step is called "deriving a solution to the problem," and here is where the usual Type I and Type II errors take place. Here you want to test one hypothesis: If you adopt this course of action to solve the problem, will it really achieve your goals?

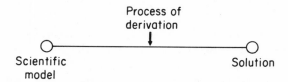

Figure 3. *The deriving phase.*

What good does it do to maximize or minimize the solution phase if the conceptualization phase was poorly handled? That is the matter we are all faced with. The crucial part of any ill-structured problem—of every one of the fundamental problems—is that of saying, "What is the problem?"

There is a last step, the step called "implementation," and that constitutes the action-taking phase of problem solving. Here you are trying to put the theoretical solution into action.

The model appears as a whole in Figure 4. Notice the line connecting the problem situation and the scientific model. This horizontal branch has traditionally been called "correspondence": the

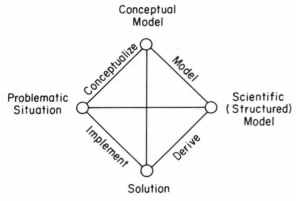

Figure 4. *The model of systemic problem solving.*

correspondence between the scientific model of the problem and the reality of the situation.

There is another kind of correspondence that we are not so familiar with. The vertical branch in Figure 4 represents the degree to which a solution corresponds to a conceptual model of a problem.

Figure 4 begins to put a perspective on the different phases of a business school. For example, courses in operations research or research methodology focus on the process of deriving solutions, while courses on change agentry focus on the implementation phase.

There is also a different form of creativity associated with every one of these phases. First, there is divergent creativity, which corresponds to the conceptualization phase. I want to produce as many conceptual alternatives as I can here. I do not want to focus or narrow them prematurely. Second is convergent creativity, which encompasses modeling and derivation. Here, I now state a problem in a precise fashion, structure it, and arrive at a solution. Finally, there is what is called political creativity, which is important to implementing the chosen solution.

In this kind of problem-solving model, you have to examine fundamental assumptions about yourself. The integrated person has not just developed one aspect of self, but all of them. I know people who spend their entire lives in one of these phases. There are those who have spent a good part of their lives deriving a solution to a particular problem in linear programming. That is a terribly important activity, but I think we have reached the point where we can no longer afford people who spend their whole career involved with just one phase.

How do you put the parts together? We have been so good in Western culture at breaking them down. Now we are faced with a question of cataclysmic proportions. How do we put the parts back together? If we do not, we may be doomed. And this putting-back-together process is what leadership is to me. A leader is a person who has psychological skills to reconcile and tolerate the antithetical. The parallel phases in Figure 4 are more than just parallel—they are really antithetical.

The dialectic

The conceptualization phase is a dialectical process. The dialectic is an organized way to explore conflict. Now either we come up with ways and methods of managing that conflict, or the game is over. Kant concludes the first critique in his *Critique of Pure Reason* with a discussion of the antimonies. Antimonies are like fundamental dialectics: "The world has a beginning in time," as opposed to "The world does not have a beginning in time." Kant saw that you could come up with an equally good argument for either one of these propositions. It was a metaphysical issue to Kant precisely because he could come up with a good pro and a con, and both made plausible sense. Where Kant stopped with identifying the conflict, Hegel began. For me this is also the beginning point—to get to a deeper reason why people disagree. In the war in Vietnam, the critical data sets were the number of enemy or the number of Americans killed, and the data by itself did not mean a thing. A hawk and a dove could both use the same data to support their respective positions. The data would never unconvince them at all. The data always supported their position, and if you are really committed to a particular world view, it always does.

Russ Ackoff has a joke that is relevant here: A guy goes into a psychiatrist's office, and he is absolutely convinced that he's dead. His problem is that he cannot convince anybody else in the world. So the psychiatrist works with this fellow for months and, unlike a real psychiatrist, he gets exasperated and says, "Hey, look. If I can prove to you that you aren't dead, will you accept this?" And the guy says, "Yes." The psychiatrist picks up a pin and says, "You don't believe dead men bleed, do you?" And the guy says, "No, dead men don't bleed." So he pricks the guy, and blood comes out. The guy looks at it and says, "Well, I'll be damned. Dead men do bleed."

We have been so committed to the world view that the S-R paradigm can explain everything because we always find supporting instances. We are all prisoners of the "dead men bleed" phenomenon, and it is very hard to give it up. One of Marshall McLuhan's best metaphors is that the fish is the last creature to discover that it is in water. None of us can conceive of ourselves outside our environment long enough to discover what our environment is like.

In a dialectic there are two world views, or a plan and a counterplan. I believe the world is inherently contradictory. I cannot conceive of any situation in the history of man for which there is just one view, and one view alone, and not an entirely plausible second view. A real dialectic is when two equally plausible positions are tugging at your soul equally at the same time.

There are assumptional sets connected to each position so that when each is coupled to the data, you reach a different set of conclusions. Dialectic is different from either deduction or induction. If you are in a deductive mode, you start with a set of assumptions held so strongly that they are really premises. You go from the premise to the data, and you arrive at a conclusion.

If you start inferentially, you work backward from your conclusion (perhaps something you observed). You couple your conclusion with the data set to derive or infer a set of general assumptions. The deduction goes down, induction goes up, but a dialectic says, "There isn't just one way of going from here to there—there are a number of ways."

A traditional dialectic splits the world in two. Both sides involve contrary assumptions, meaning that if one is true, the other is false. But they both could be false. They are exclusive, but not

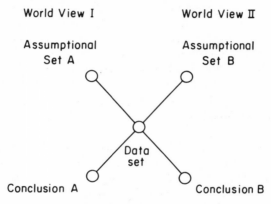

Figure 5. The dialectic.

exhaustive. Pro-abortion and anti-abortion positions do not exhaust all the alternatives. There are many varieties of pro-abortion and many varieties of anti-abortion. What is hoped for, by having people go through a dialectic, is that they will be tempted, if not induced, to come up with another world view that will be broader than either of the two original world views.

In a dialectic, the purpose is not to change the actors' world views, because they never talk to one another. They are so locked into their views that the amount of information that goes back and forth is zero. The purpose of the dialectic, then, is for the uncommitted. Hopefully they can come up with a new world view that synthesizes the two positions.

A former fellow graduate student, Dick Mason, was able to

engage in such a dialectic in a major corporation. The members of the organization were dissatisfied because none of the traditional strategic planning methods worked. They could not build a mathematical model because they were divided on all the fundamental premises that have to be resolved before model building can occur. So they brought in Mason, and he attempted to identify two groups of managers who had conflicting points of view but who did not know what the source of the conflict was. He tried to get them to examine their basic underlying assumptions and ex-pose to them what the real source of the disagreement was. What he did was shape their world views into opposing basic propositions, so that for every fundamental assumption characterizing one element of this world view, there was an opposing assumption characterizing an element of that world view. The basic assumptions were so basic that they seemed almost trivial once they were examined, but they had snarled the organization.

The dialectical process and leadership

What kind of leadership does the lesson of the dialectic imply? A leader needs more than just a little touch with reality, more than the reality of a single vision. The leader must know the limitations, the defects, and the strengths of several visions. Let me summarize how this might look with two different types of managers—the reactive (traditional) manager and the learning manager who follows the theory of problem solving.

1. The reactive manager reacts by repeating previously successful response patterns—he goes back to dredge up things that worked in the past. The learning manager, in contrast, does not react. He innovates by reflecting and then creating original response patterns.

2. The reactive manager responds by viewing the variables and dimensions of the situation within the context of a given habitual frame of reference; more often than not, it is a single frame of reference. The learning manager views the situation from at least two independent frames of reference, at least one of which is unique to the situation. This helps him get a subjective assessment of the Type III error.

3. The reactive manager may test many alternatives, but always within a single frame of reference—similar to the engineers who were going to either put in a new elevator or speed up the old elevators. That is still within a single frame of reference—a technological one. The learning manager will test several alternatives within multiple frames of reference.

4. The reactive manager seeks to maintain the organization's values and patterns of internal relationships exactly as he found them. This process is what Schon (1971) calls "dynamic conservatism." The learning manager is willing to modify, even to destroy, some central aspects of the organization's boundaries and patterns of relations so he can construct new ones.

5. The reactive manager reacts instinctively to the data presented to him. The learning manager engages in controlled activity, experiments, and otherwise pursues data that are meaningful within multiple frames of reference and can be used to construct new and useful relationships. The learning manager is more concerned with hypothesis generation.

6. The reactive manager relies exclusively on conscious, rational thinking. The learning manager innovates by use of the unconscious—the irrational and, even less understood, the nonrational. (Jung identified the nonrational, that never-never land of the mind.) The learning manager inevitably has to go into the unconscious, the irrational, and the humorous to gain new meaning and perspective.

What I am saying is that, for me, the learning manager is the hero. And there are not many heroes in organizations or in the social sciences.

In many cases we will have to make new myths. The old myths are crumbling. All the old institutions of our society have been under attack. You cannot name one, including family, church, government, and science—supposedly the most rational one of all —upon which we would place our basic beliefs. What we need is to provide ways of combining rather than separating some of these institutions. I think *that* was the original sin—separating them. We have to reintegrate our institutions and our sciences, and this takes a broad vision, not a reactive, reductionist one.

References

Ackoff, R. L. *Redesigning the future: A systems approach to societal problems.* New York: Wiley, 1974.

Duhem, P. [*The aim and structure of physical theory*] (P. P. Weiner, Trans.). Princeton, N.J.: Princeton University Press, 1954. Also New York: Atheneum, 1962. (Originally published, 1914.)

Koestler, A. *The sleep walkers: A history of man's changing vision of the universe.* New York: Macmillan, 1959.

Mitroff, I. I. *The subjective side of science: A philosophical enquiry into the psychology of the Apollo moon scientists.* New York: American Elsevier, 1974.

Pirsig, R. M. *Zen and the art of motorcycle maintenance: An inquiry into values.* New York: Morrow, 1974.

Schon, D. A. *Beyond the stable state.* New York: Random House, 1971.

Westfall, R. Newton and the fudge factor. *Science,* 1973. **179,** 751–758.

Commentary

Mitroff explicitly captured the dominant theme of this book when he cautioned against error of the third kind—solving the wrong problems precisely. While leadership is not the only area in social science (or even physical science) to be caught in Type III errors, it has suffered enormously from what Maslow has called "means-centered science." Without adequately coping with definitional issues or with conceptual expansion, empirical research in leadership quickly focused on the deductive model of hypothesis testing. Pfeffer has recounted some major problems with leadership research, and Weick, Lundberg, Pondy, Vaill, and Mitroff have explored many conceptual and methodological alternatives. This, in essence, is the message of this book: There has been no real dialectic in leadership, but it is not too late. As social scientists we do have more than one methodology for collecting and analyzing data, and there are many different ways to approach the briar patch of leadership.

In the next chapter, Pondy and Mitroff provide a perspective on the chapters of this book and extend its message to broader issues in science. Science does not have to be as Maslow described it, "a technique whereby noncreative people can create." Most of the topics in social science are inherently interesting—we all live with, conjecture about and, in a personal way, are experts on leadership. A science that takes an interesting topic and makes it dull needs to stop and look at itself. Scientists (and leaders) are not just technicians. The numbers and the designs have little meaning if there is none of the phenomenon left when the answer is found.

MWM

8. Afterthoughts on the Leadership Conference

Ian I. Mitroff
and Louis R. Pondy

Reflecting on the meaning of the conference, we have concluded that its importance is not simply the proposal of new and creative approaches to leadership. In fact, that limited interpretation may blind us to a greater significance. We are conditioned by our scientific training to associate progress with greater rigor, greater precision, disintegrative analysis, more empirical documentation of a phenomenon, and the progressive exorcism of value-laden questions in favor of a purer pursuit of "truth," that is, a closer and closer fitting of our theories to the one objective reality we presume exists. Further, we accept as an acid test of such progress that social consensus (viz., the replicability criterion) be established. But these indicators of progress are misleading. They may be appropriate for measuring progress *within* a paradigm, but they cannot begin to describe progress that results from a paradigm shift. And we believe that the real significance of the conference is that it belongs and adds momentum to the embryo of a revolution in organizational behavior, and perhaps in the whole of the social sciences.

A key element of this revolution is a greater tolerance for imprecision and "nonrigor" (Isn't it interesting that we have no nonpejorative antonym for "rigor" in our language?) and for the use of "distant" metaphors in our inquiry. Consider Lundberg's conversation with Dr. Hypothetical (and his use of metaphors during his workshop to communicate about leadership); or Weick's playful thinking about a pattern maker as a source of hypotheses about mediums; or Vaill's references to poetry and music and his use of sports as an organizational metaphor. We think that not enough attention was paid to how the speakers went about their craft and how the other participants responded. Perhaps because it was so much a part of all we did, we never noticed it. What is remarkable is that no one felt compelled to apologize for or criticize the absence of hard data, or reliability indices, or factor loadings—partly because we were busy generating ideas. And if you are spinning off ideas, you are allowed to be intuitive and nonrigorous, so long as you get scientific again when you begin testing the ideas empirically. Rigor can take a holiday, so long as it is *only* a holiday.

But we believe that the revolution's increased openness toward imprecision extends *beyond* the hypothesis generation stage. This is not to say that precise, rigorous, empirically testable descriptions and theories are out. But it does mean that looser, non-testable, nongeneralizable descriptions (e.g., poems) of social facts are equally legitimate forms of representation and perhaps, as we shall shortly argue, even more appropriate forms of inquiry than the normal model of science.

Surely, at this point, some readers will begin to regard our extension of the intuitive mode to the final stages of scientific inquiry, and to its end product as well, as a rebellious act inconsistent with the very essence of science. Scientific inquiry has succeeded when all relevant facts about a phenomenon are made public and explicit, when they are raised from the "object" level, past the metaphorical level, to the level of symbolic dialogue. But perhaps "science" is the wrong strategy for understanding social phenomena!

Science is a low-variety "medium" (to use Weick's term). It proceeds conservatively to minimize the chance of accepting a false fact as representative of reality. Its capacity to process variety is limited by numerous internal demands for logic (e.g., two contradictory assertions cannot both be true) and empiricism (e.g., tests of statistical significance). But—and this is a key point in the argument—if a low-variety medium is used to register a high-variety phenomenon, then a long period of time will be required for the complete registration to take place.

Now what do we mean by a "long period of time"—relative to what? Suppose we use the lifetime of a phenomenon as our measuring stick. The lifetime of phenomena described by the laws of motion is assumed to be infinite. No serious physicist thinks relativistic effects are "new"; they simply had not been discovered before Einstein. So far as we know, physical phenomena *at the level* of Newton's and Einstein's laws are not evolving, although perhaps our understanding of them is. But *at the level* of our inquiry into social phenomena, evolution surely is taking place, not the least important source being our current knowledge and theories of behavior. Now—*and this is the crux of the argument*—if a low-variety medium with a long convergence time is applied to a high-variety phenomenon with a short lifetime, then the phenomenon will never be completely described or understood before it vanishes and some new phenomenon supplants it. That is the guts of our conjecture that *science is the wrong inquiring system for the social "sciences"; it converges too slowly relative to the rate of decay and evolution of social phenomena.*

What we saw happening at the Greensboro conference was the implicit forming of that conjecture and the application of it to the field of leadership. And we believe it is an important (perhaps the most important) part of the revolution in organizational and social behavior.

We would like to comment on two other points related to the expressed doubt about science as an inquiring strategy. One has to do with alternatives to "analysis" as a means of understanding something. The second deals with the role of values in research.

Analysis works by breaking a thing into parts small enough to be understood. But the essence of a social system is its configuration, and decomposing it destroys the very thing we are attempting to understand. So analysis is not an acceptable strategy of inquiry for social phenomena. (Note that analytical thinking is the guts of most scientific inquiry—e.g., the most admired experiments are those that control all variables but the ones [ideally, *one*] under investigation.)

But if analysis is unsuitable, what alternative strategy both preserves the configurational integrity of a social system and yields understanding of its nature? It is a difficult question because we have been so conditioned to think of the analytical model of inquiry as the only acceptable one. The question was actually raised at the conference, during Peter Vaill's presentation, but not dealt with. It took us some time to even begin to know how to generate alternatives to analysis. How can you understand something except by taking it apart?!

We would like to propose a resolution to this paradox. Analysis proceeds by *de*composing a phenomenon *downward* into parts. We offer the alternative of *com*posing the phenomenon *upward* with its conjugate or correlative phenomena. Metaphorically, this is like giving "dancing partners" to the phenomenon. Different characteristics of the phenomenon are projected on or brought out by each of its partners. To understand leadership, we should let it waltz with problem solving, and language, and technology, and "mediums"—the more the better. This is precisely what the speakers at the conference were doing and why understanding of leadership seemed to leap forward. (It is interesting to note that chemistry, before it was invaded by physics, proceeded compositionally. To understand the behavior of oxygen, chemists composed it with carbon, and iron, and hydrogen, and. . . .) So we propose composition as a strategy of inquiry more appropriate to social and organizational behavior than analysis.

Values play no role in scientific analysis. Long ago the Greeks subordinated the search for the Good to the search for the Truth. In Robert Pirsig's (1974) words:

> The reality of the Good, represented by Sophists, and the reality of the True, represented by the dialecticians, were engaged in a huge struggle for the future mind of man. Truth won, the Good lost, and that is why today we have so little difficulty accepting the reality of Truth and so much difficulty accepting the reality of Quality, even though there is no more agreement in one area than in the other. [p. 365]

The social sciences have been engaged in a massive effort to understand human systems by treating them "objectively," that is, as if they were things rather than people. It is interesting to observe that "objectively" has the same root as the word "objection." "To object" is to offer a reason or argument *in opposition.* Thus, to treat a human system "objectively" is to stand in opposition to it, to treat it as inherently different from the observers, and in particular to divest it of values, because values have to do with what might be, not what is, and therefore cannot be observed dispassionately as part of the objective truth. Here we surely invite charges of heresy—to question the *value* (!) of objectivity. (The dog of value comes back to bite the hand of science after all.) To understand a social system, the values of its members *and of the observer* must be explicitly recognized. This is a central part of what Geoffrey Vickers (1968) has called an "appreciation" of a problem situation.

Casting doubt on the relevance of objectivity, analysis, and rigorous science to social inquiry forms the basis, we believe, for the coming revolution. The seeds of doubt were sown in Greensboro. We hope we have contributed to an awareness of the significance of what happened there.

References

Pirsig, R. M. *Zen and the art of motorcycle maintenance.* New York: Bantam, 1974.

Vickers, G. *The art of judgment* (Part I). New York: Basic Books, 1968.

9. Where Else Can We Go?

Morgan W. McCall, Jr., and Michael M. Lombardo

> It is no light matter to make up one's mind about any-
> thing, even about sea-otters, and once made up it is even
> harder to abandon the position. When a hypothesis is
> deeply accepted it becomes a growth which only a kind
> of surgery can amputate. [Steinbeck, 1962, p. 180]

After years of study it would be comforting to believe that we
know a lot about leadership. It is difficult to go back to basic
assumptions and entertain the notion that major surgery may be
necessary for the study of leadership. Stogdill's (1974) stocktaking
and inventory of results has shown that the accumulated data,
even when pulled together, are still contradictory, ambiguous,
and narrow. Improvement of our understanding of leadership
apparently does not lie in pursuing existing trends or in attempting
to integrate existing research. Conceptually and methodologically,
leadership research has bogged down.

The authors of this book have tried to redirect thinking about
leadership and scientific inquiry by offering alternative conceptual
frameworks, by identifying potentially useful but neglected variables, and by exploring methodologies that have not been adequately used.

Conceptual issues

What kinds of assumptions have been made about leadership that
might bear closer scrutiny?

Pfeffer surfaced a major issue by postulating that sometimes
leadership does not matter. His point, that environmental factors

often influence organizational outcomes much more than organizational leadership, highlights at least two facets of leadership. The first is that we seldom examine leadership at high levels in the organization—the level of leadership where organizational impact is most likely. While we have innumerable studies of first-level supervisors, army squads, and small groups of college students, we have little data on the leadership behavior of corporate presidents, chief executives, boards of directors, cabinets, or the like. It is not surprising that the models we have built work best for lower-level leadership. The assumption made is that leadership is much the same regardless of level in the organization, which includes differences in task, structure, technology, position power, etc.

The second facet to which Pfeffer calls attention is the importance of large-scale contextual factors such as the economy, competition, regulatory agencies, politics, budgets, and labor unions. For all of our situations and contingencies, for all our talk about leadership and environmental influences, there is a devastating lack of systematic research on the relationship between specific, potent elements of the environment and the behavior of leaders. Even lower-level managers are aware of, process, and use information about these macro-level forces (McCall, 1974), and such forces no doubt play a crucial causal role in such "situational" conditions as leader-member relations, position power of the leader, group cohesion, productivity, and job satisfaction.

When Mitroff suggested that we have studied well-structured problems when, in fact, important problems are more typically ill-structured, he extended Pfeffer's implicit theme. How leaders *and* researchers deal with lack of structure is a basic problem in current leadership research. Weick's application of requisite variety and Vaill's analysis of typical assumptions made by organizational researchers pinpoint the intersection of researcher and researched. Perhaps we are interested in leaders, not because of their "incremental influence over subordinates," but because of their incremental influence in solving ill-structured problems in ill-structured situations. To understand such behavior, the researcher must apply research tools suitable to the ill-structured phenomenon under study. Thus, the problems with leadership research are not based solely on the complexity of leadership but also involve the scientific models used to study it.

The complex relationship between phenomenon and research methods extends beyond organizational behavior into areas of training (of leaders and researchers), scientific inquiry, philosophy, and professional disciplines. The message? Simply stated, we need to take stock of our science—reexamine where we are and how we got there. Science is not ahistorical; myths and traditions exist in science just as they do in organizations and societies. When a field of scientific study, such as leadership, reaches an impasse, it is time to examine its most cherished assumptions and deepest foundations. Such examination inevitably exposes cracks that may represent a threat to the whole structure. But it also reveals alternatives to the present course of events and may represent a potential paradigm shift (Kuhn, 1970).

The primary conceptual shift suggested in this book is the reversal of the reductionist strategy in leadership and social science research. Leadership research has prematurely focused on the deductive, hypothesis-testing model before conceptualization of the phenomenon has been adequately explored. The ambiguity of the term leadership, the untested assumptions, the mixed research results, the proliferation of unintegratable models, and the abundance of Type III errors are all symptoms of a larger, more basic problem. Mitroff suggested that social science has followed a model of physical science that never existed to solve problems that are, at least at this time, not amenable to physical science techniques.

Whatever the genesis of the present turmoil in leadership, the authors of this book converge on the central theme of systems thinking about leadership. Moving beyond the catchwords and glitter of the systems concept, this book suggests that leadership has no meaning outside the context—the "it"—in which it is embedded. Lundberg and Pondy seriously questioned the meaning and appropriateness of the word leadership for the wide variety of phenomena encompassed by it. A major flaw in much of the existing research results from studying leadership for its own sake in the limited context of leader-follower relations. "Leadering" only makes sense when viewed as "leadering for what?" Looking at the criteria most often employed by leadership researchers—*group* productivity, *group* absenteeism and turnover, *group* satisfaction—one might get the impression that improving the immediate follower group's performance is all that leading is about. What if the group is the most stable part of the leader's environment? What if group productivity and satisfaction are relatively constant? What if leader-member relationships are established fairly quickly and remain stable? Maybe the real essence of leadership lies in the leader's ability to deal with non-followers —the countless peers, colleagues, bosses, associates, and key people who occupy positions in other units or outside organizations that directly influence the group's ability to do its job. What are the criteria for leadership when there are no readily identifiable followers? Leaders in ideas are one example—who is in Aristotle's work group? When we study presidents, are we going to restrict our criteria to outcomes of the Cabinet and immediate subordinates?

The conceptual underpinnings of the approach to leadership developed in this book can be summarized as follows:

1. Leader-member relations are only one part, and perhaps a small part, of the leadership phenomenon.

2. Leaders and organizations are full of contradictions and antithetical elements. Incongruities and non sequiturs are common, not rare. It is bizarre to expect a leader to have one "style," or one goal, or one task.

3. Leaders may face an infinite variety of specific situations and engage in an infinite variety of overt behaviors. Trying to generate enough contingencies to explain all possible combinations of situations and behaviors may be fruitless. On the other hand, exploring deeper levels (Pondy's analogy to linguistics, Weick's content-free media, Vaill's "it") may provide sensible answers. After all, leaders face these complex situations and somehow function. How do they enact their own environments? How do they select behaviors? How do they solve ill-structured problems?

4. Organizations, situations, and individuals are constantly changing (Weick's loosely coupled systems, Vaill's dynamic optimiza-

tion, Mitroff's ill-structured problems, Lundberg's expectations and coalitions). To say, as Fiedler (1967) does, that leaders should be fitted to the situation is to deny reality.

5. The immediate situation in which leadership occurs is only important in the context of the larger situation. Macro forces (such as politics and economics) are important in shaping the immediate situation, as are myths and traditions that pervade organizations and societies. Attributions to leaders are as much a part of the leadership process as what leaders actually do.

These conceptual underpinnings have significant implications for leadership training. Weick said that we are going to have to see what leaders do on-line, whether the line is a real or a simulated one. A review of the training literature revealed only two organizations, the Center for Creative Leadership and the U.S. Army Research Institute for the Behavioral and Social Sciences (Olmstead, Cleary, Lackey, & Salter, 1973), that have used complex organizational simulations highlighting the multitudinous and sometimes capricious demands of organizations. These simulations dealt with a variety of ill-structured problems within a total system approach. Another possible training vehicle is a behavioral in-basket, where trainees respond first to typical in-basket situations, then face these situations under simulated conditions.

J. R. Gibb (1974) sums up the need for an integrated systems view in a statement about T-group and encounter-group training that is echoed in other reviews of general management and human relations training: "[They] are ineffective unless they are integrated into long-range efforts that include such elements as a total organizational focus, system-wide data collection, provision for feedback and information flow, organization-focused consultation over an extended time and data-supported theory" (p. 160).

The authors did not present a unified, tidy conceptualization, but rather a loosely coupled framework to guide thinking about leadership. More important, they addressed leadership as the truly complex phenomenon it is. Rejecting the comfortable strategy of trying to understand the whole by knowing about the parts, they have said, "If you can't understand the phenomenon as it really is, forget it."

Rather than "forget it," however, the authors have suggested both variables and methodologies congruent with their loose conceptual frameworks.

Neglected variables and concepts in leadership

It was suggested that effective leaders may be docile at times, that their activity level must be congruent with the demands of the group and the particular task, and that they actively arrange and rearrange their environments. Studies of managerial success based on assessment center research support the contention that energy and activity are important variables (e.g., Wollowick & McNamara, 1969), and Mintzberg's (1973) description of the managerial job documents the demanding nature of the leadership role. Not only do leaders engage in dozens of different activities in a day, but 50 percent of these activities last nine minutes or less (Mintzberg, 1973). Characterized by brevity, variety, and fragmentation, the job of leading demands a lot of energy.

Clearly, sheer activity is not the only element of leadership, but we know very little about its place in the process.

Myths and traditions were discussed in several contexts, primarily that their utility for understanding organizations and leadership processes has been overlooked. In spite of numerous comments that "past behavior is the best predictor of future behavior," leadership research has been strikingly devoid of longitudinal investigations. (Graen's model, Graen & Cashman, 1976, pp. 143–165, is an exception to the rule.) Myth and tradition represent an institutionalization of the past and, therefore, have explanatory potential. Our myths about leadership and heroes, which abruptly surfaced in Lundberg's workshop, not only influence the behavior of individuals in leadership roles, but also affect the followers' attributions and expectations.

Steinbeck's (1962) discussion of sea monster myths captures the potential of the concept:

They so wanted it to be a sea-serpent. Even we hoped it would be. When sometime a true sea-serpent, complete and undecayed, is found or caught, a shout of triumph will go through the world. "There, you see," men will say, "I knew they were there all the time. . . ." Men really need sea-monsters in their personal oceans. . . . If the Old Man of the Sea should turn out to be some great malformed sea-lion, a lot of people would feel a sharp personal loss—a Santa Claus loss. [p. 31]

When people are asked to list great leaders, they inevitably mention Kennedy, Churchill, Gandhi, Hitler, and others of their status. Most of them are dead and have the advantage of historical retrospect—they have become mythical. The qualities ascribed to them—eloquence, charisma, power, forcefulness—are all part of the superhero image we have about leadership. To suggest for a moment that the myths and traditions about leadership do not affect leader behavior or the ways leaders are perceived by others is to neglect an important reality.

Several variables suggested in this book pertain to relationships between "leadering" and the specific task requirements faced. Mitroff addressed the strategies required to handle ill-structured problems, Weick applied the concept of requisite variety to the leader's ability to understand the environment, and Vaill talked about leaders processing more information than do their followers. Researchers have addressed leadership and cognitive style (e.g., Mitchell, 1970; Gruenfeld, 1970, pp. 44–53; Hill, 1969) and have found a few moderately significant relationships. Typically, such research is based on cognitive measures obtained by tests (such as the Hidden Figures Test) and fails to consider the situational context. Information processing studies that include environmental referents (e.g., Schroder, Driver, & Streufert, 1967) have produced much more convincing results. A central problem with applying cognitive constructs to leadership is, as Vaill pointed out, that much of the effective leader's action is intuitive, affective, and value-laden. Leaders, like skilled craftsmen, work by "feel." While complex cognitive maps are probably essential for effective leadership, they may be subconscious or disorganized—and therefore not measurable by conventional tests. To the extent that the environment is disorganized, disorganized cognitive representations may be more accurate. Thus, the person who can delineate all the causal paths, who knows how everything influences everything else, is inevitably reducing his or her media qualities.

Another major set of variables worthy of consideration is Lundberg's notion of shadows and lieutenants. Much of the leadership research investigates single leaders (or at best formal and informal leaders) and their groups of subordinates. Yet studies of subordinate feedback have indicated that subordinates perceive several influential leaders in their task environment (e.g., Dornbusch & Scott, 1975). Couple this formal structure of multiple leaders with the individual leader's own shadows and lieutenants, and the leader-group paradigm becomes inadequate.

Delegation, for example, is generally considered to be a strategy of participative management. What a delegative leader may be doing is forming a loyal coalition, generating a sounding board, and/or redistributing power and influence. A leadership researcher may see delegation activity as a leadership style and correlate it with group productivity, while, in many cases, delegation is a political tool used by leaders to create a desirable situation.

Both Weick and Vaill discussed perceptions of time in relation to leadership. Jaques's (1961) work on the time span of discretion suggests the usefulness of a temporal variable, and Weick and Vaill extend the notion. For Weick a good medium operates on a shorter time horizon, and for Vaill the nature of the system influences a participant's time perceptions. Much of an organization's activity is time-referenced: anticipating new technologies, developing future leadership, keeping adequate inventories, planning for market fluctuations, preparing for new laws and regulations. The temporal aspect of leadership has to be important.

Another set of neglected variables includes the leader's use of language. What kinds of special languages develop in organizations? How much overlap is there between the personal codings of leaders and subordinates? Is it true that a "real" leader makes sense of things and communicates that sense in ways that others can understand? Assessment center research supports the importance of "communication skills" to managerial success (e.g., Bray & Grant, 1966), but it has not answered the crucial question of how these skills are important.

Other studies (e.g., Jago & Vroom, 1976, pp. 103–120) have

shown that leaders' descriptions of their own behavior do not coincide with the descriptions of followers. We might conclude (a) that the instrument was invalid, (b) that either the self-report or the subordinate report was biased or wrong, or (c) that subordinates observe only one aspect of the leader's total behavior. What if the disparity between leader and follower reports has its roots in language and communication? Perhaps leaders and followers have different symbols and meanings that they attach to behavior and to words. Perhaps limited overlap is responsible for the lack of coincidence, and perhaps communication and language are important leadership tools.

Several approaches to leadership have considered the relationship between leader behavior and subordinate expectations (e.g., House, 1971; Evans, 1970), but few have considered the impact of self-expectation on leader behavior. Lundberg's thesis can be extended to reverse the trend of dwelling on leadership as it affects *subordinate* outcomes. How do subordinates affect *leader* satisfaction, motivation, and effectiveness? How do these in turn affect the leader's behavior?

Vaill's comment on the importance of leader expertise in high-performing systems opens another intriguing avenue for leadership research. Social scientists, in focusing on general variables that apply to "all" leaders, have virtually ignored the technical competence variable in leadership. Training courses based on social science emphasize interpersonal skills, leadership style, environmental/structural/situational factors, small group dynamics, motivation, etc., but seldom do they address the issue of expertise. Researchers often link leadership style to subordinate performance without considering the leader's technical competence to perform his/her own job or that of the group. Take, for example, David Ogilvy's (1965) description of a head chef. Among other characteristics, the head chef (1) ruled with an iron rod, (2) did not tolerate mistakes, (3) flaunted his inequitable income, (4) inspected every single dish, and (5) seldom praised anyone. While most normative leadership theories would lead us to expect all manner of dissatisfaction among group members, the "esprit de corps" of his kitchen "would have done credit to the marines." A key factor in this tyrant's leadership? "He was the best cook in the whole brigade, and we knew it" (p. 199).

These and other variables suggested in this book represent a domain of neglected issues. Almost all of these variables involve context factors that require the researcher to know something about the "it" of leadership. Almost all of the variables are linked to processes and thus force the researcher out of a static paradigm. None of the variables is presented as the single determinant of leadership behavior.

The value of exploring these neglected variables is intimately linked with the conceptualizing process. That so many variables have been overlooked suggests that the leadership well is not yet dry—in spite of the thousands of studies already done (see Stogdill, 1974). It is encouraging to see that the loose conceptual frameworks advanced here can spawn further studies that can extend in so many new directions.

Methodology

If we accept Mitroff's view that social scientists, and especially leadership researchers, have emphasized finding solutions without identifying the problems, we are forced to examine seriously our methodological suitcase. Sophisticated research designs are aimed at hypothesis testing and therefore assume there is an hypothesis. What methods are available for discovering the problem?

Weick summed it up by calling for unstatistical naturalism among differentiating generalists—a call for a new generation of John Steinbecks and Charles Darwins. The aim of such research is to *see* what is going on. Vaill suggests that you study a system you know well so you can identify a change—feel it, as the system members do. As Heinlein (1968) has put it, "'Grok' means to understand so thoroughly that the observer becomes part of the observed . . ." (p. 206). Grokking, in Heinlein's sense, is essentially a juxtaposition of opposites—it means love *and* hate. To understand something fully, you must see its many antithetical facets; you must love it and hate it.

Hypothesis generation can also result from playfulness, as Lundberg described and actually showed. The dialectical process, described by Mitroff, provides another technique for generating new "world views" and discovering hidden assumptions. So does emulating other research paradigms than those used by the physical sciences (such as those of linguistics).

All the techniques advocated, from studying poetry to participant observation, share the common goal of resisting reductionistic
thinking. It is probably not true that you must have been a leader
to study leadership (any more than a biologist must have been a
crab to study marine biology), but it is probably true that a
leadership researcher who has never seen a leader will have some
trouble depicting reality. The key for researchers such as Wil-
liam F. Whyte, Peter Blau, Leonard Sayles, Philip Selznick, and
others is not that any of them ever headed an organization, but
that they went into organizations to *look* at what was going on.
They had the skill that Pondy described of leaders—to make sense
of something and then communicate that sense in a way that
others could understand.

Any advocacy of observational and anthropological methods
immediately generates two counterarguments: (1) You cannot
generalize from a case study, and (2) observers are biased, and
experimental designs reduce bias.

Let us take the latter argument first. Obviously, experimental
designs are useful, especially for studying the effects of a powerful, measurable variable—usually cognitive or structural or anything that can be objectified. Statements that case studies are im-
pure because they are subject to observer bias are suspect on
several points. A case study involves looking at a complete system,
and systems are both rational and irrational, subjective and
objective, random and purposive, cognitive and affective. The
system is being observed by a person who has the same characteristics. To single out objective aspects is to cut with an ax, then
slice with a micronome. The very cutting and slicing is value-laden
—it involves chopping up complex people with complex psychological makeups who interact within equally complex systems; this
is one reason why physical science and social science are light-
years apart. Unlike water, people do not usually boil at 212°F.

There are certainly objective and some subjective elements of
a system that can and should be studied. But they are not the
system. They cannot explain it. They *illuminate* underlying relationships and meanings that we, with our limited information-
processing capabilites, could never see without the use of statistics.
The broader picture of the system is what "differentiating generalists" are needed for. Their role is not unlike that of the "new
journalists" who are basically saying, "Here are my values and,

given these values, here is the way I see this system." But differentiating generalists can go far beyond this by using experimental and case methods to complement one another. Weick makes the point that a researcher's (or a leader's) tools of analysis have to be as complicated as the system he is up against. The researcher's requisite variety has to equal the system's, and in some respects, what Weick calls requisite variety is what a lot of other people call observer bias.

As for the criticism that a case study cannot be generalized, we may be asking the wrong question. In the first place, do we want to generalize? One major problem with leadership research and its teleological methods is that it has been generalized prematurely. Barely significant Ps, Fs, and X^2s do not necessarily warrant generalization, nor do carefully controlled laboratory experiments. Large samples are seldom chosen randomly, correlations do not prove causality, sophisticated multivariate techniques do not enhance the validity of crude measurements, precise answers to the wrong questions do not help. The real issue is not generalizing, but matching the scientific techniques to the state of the science. In leadership research particularly, where there is little agreement on definitions and concepts, the emphasis should be on finding the right questions. Later, perhaps, the generalized answers can be found within hypothesis-testing paradigms.

A sense of perspective

The conference on which this book was based was created out of a sense of frustration and a common belief that leadership research has been disappointingly empty. This is not to say that nothing has been learned about leadership in the forty or more years that it has been a topic of empirical study. We can say with some confidence that personality traits alone are not good predictors of leadership effectiveness (e.g., C. A. Gibb, 1969, pp. 205–282). We can say that a leader's consideration toward subordinates generally is correlated with their satisfaction (though the direction of the causal arrow remains in doubt). We can say with assurance that leadership is a situational phenomenon and that no particular style or approach will be effective in all situations. We can account for about 20 percent of the variance in managerial success by knowing how a person performs in an assessment center (Howard, 1974). We know that leaders play a crucial role by structuring the expectations of their followers (House, 1971; Evans, 1970). These are not trivial statements, and our knowledge of leadership is, in most respects, no more primitive than our understanding of human motivation or organizational design or economics.

Nonetheless, leadership remains more of a performing art (Vaill, 1974) than a science. It may be destined to remain so; perhaps to our ultimate benefit. But there are other ways to approach understanding this slippery topic, and this book has suggested a potpourri of concepts, variables, and methodologies that might help researchers.

The increasing number of researchers expressing concerns with leadership research, past and present, is an encouraging sign. Symposia at professional meetings (e.g., Ned Rosen, Chair, *Some Neglected Aspects of Research on Leadership in Formal Organizations,* American Psychological Association, 1974; Ralph Stogdill, Chair, *What's NOT Happening in Leadership Research,* Academy of Management, 1975) have generated options and opened new directions. Still "Leadership, where else can we go?" is an open question.

"Would you tell me, please, which way I ought to go from here?"

"That depends a good deal on where you want to get to," said the Cat.

"I don't much care where—" said Alice.

"Then it doesn't matter which way you go," said the Cat.

"—so long as I get *somewhere,*" Alice added as an explanation.

"Oh, you're sure to do that," said the Cat, "if you only walk long enough."

[From Lewis Carroll's *Alice's Adventures in Wonderland*]

References

Bray, D. W., & Grant, D. L. The assessment center in the measurement of potential for business management. *Psychological Monographs,* 1966, **80** (17, Whole No. 625).

Dornbusch, S. M., & Scott, W. R. *Evaluation and the exercise of authority.* Washington, D.C.: Jossey-Bass, 1975.

Evans, M. The effects of supervisory behavior on the path-goal relationship. *Organizational Behavior and Human Performance,* 1970, **5,** 277–298.

Fiedler, F. E. *A theory of leadership effectiveness.* New York: McGraw-Hill, 1967.

Gibb, C. A. Leadership. In G. Lindzey & E. Aronson (Eds.), *The handbook of social psychology* (Vol. 4, 2nd ed.). Reading, Mass.: Addison-Wesley, 1969.

Gibb, J. R. The message from research. In J. W. Pfeiffer & J. E. Jones (Eds.), *The 1974 annual handbook for group facilitators.* La Jolla, Calif.: University Associates, 1974.

Graen, G., & Cashman, J. F. A role-making model of leadership in formal organizations: A developmental approach. In J. G. Hunt & L. L. Larson (Eds.), *Leadership frontiers.* Kent, Ohio: Kent State University Press, 1976.

Gruenfeld, L. W. Cognitive style—field dependence-independence as a framework for the study of task and social orientations in organizational leadership. In B. M. Bass, R. Cooper, & J. A. Haas (Eds.), *Managing for accomplishment.* Lexington, Mass.: Heath Lexington, 1970.

Heinlein, R. A. *Stranger in a strange land.* New York: Berkeley Publishing, 1968.

Hill, W. The LPC leader: A cognitive twist. *Academy of Management Proceedings,* 1969, **29,** 125–130.

House, R. J. A path-goal theory of leader effectiveness. *Administrative Science Quarterly,* 1971, **16,** 321–338.

Howard, A. An assessment of assessment centers. *Academy of Management Journal,* 1974, **17,** 115–134.

Jago, A. G., & Vroom, V. H. Perceptions of leadership style: Superior and subordinate descriptions of decision-making behavior. In J. G. Hunt & L. L. Larson (Eds.), *Leadership frontiers.* Kent, Ohio: Kent State University Press, 1976.

Jaques, E. *Equitable payment.* New York: Wiley, 1961.

Kuhn, T. S. *The structure of scientific revolutions* (Vol. 2, No. 2, 2nd ed.), *International Encyclopedia of Unified Science.* Chicago: University of Chicago Press, 1970.

McCall, M. W., Jr. The perceived informational environment of formal leaders (Doctoral dissertation, Cornell University, 1974). *Dissertation Abstracts International*, 1975, **35**, 4244-B. (University Microfilms No. 75–4259)

Mintzberg, H. *The nature of managerial work.* New York: Harper & Row, 1973.

Mitchell, T. B. Leader complexity and leadership style. *Journal of Personality and Social Psychology*, 1970, **16**, 166–174.

Ogilvy, D. The creative chef. In G. Steiner (Ed.), *The creative organization*. Chicago: University of Chicago Press, 1965.

Olmstead, J. A., Cleary, F. K., Lackey, L. L., & Salter, J. A. *Development of leadership assessment simulations* (HumRRO Technical Report 13–21). Alexandria, Va.: Human Resources Research Organization, September 1973. (NTIS No. AD 772 990)

Schroder, H. M., Driver, M. J., & Streufert, S. *Human information processing.* New York: Holt, Rinehart and Winston, 1967.

Steinbeck, J. *The log from the Sea of Cortez.* New York: Viking, 1962.

Stogdill, R. *Handbook of leadership.* New York: Free Press, 1974.

Vaill, P. B. *On the general theory of management.* Paper presented at the meeting of the Society for Humanistic Management, Washington, D.C., November 19, 1974.

Wollowick, H. B., & McNamara, W. J. Relationship of the components of an assessment center to management progress. *Journal of Applied Psychology*, 1969, **53**, 343–352.

Name Index

Subject Index

Power, 14, 20
Problem solving: in organizations,
51–52; and time horizons, 51–52.
See also Systemic problem solving
Problems, and structure, 131, 152
Promotion, 17–18, 24–25. *See also*
Selection process

Reductionistic thinking, in research,
153, 161
Requisite variety, 41–44; and
contour gauge, 41; and medium,
57; and loose coupling, 57–58
Research: problems in, xii, 80–81,
121–125, 126; criticism of, 3–7,
59–60, 63, 162; leadership in
organizations, 5–6, 116–117;
neglected variables, 10, 84–85,
156–160; and structure, 10–11,
100; conceptual issues, 10–11, 151,
154–160; overview, 13–29; of
organizational performance, 13,
104–106, 115–116, 121–125, 126;
and spines, 37–60; and contour
gauge, 37–42, 46; of social influence, 91–92; linguistics prototype, 96–98; assumptions, 104–106,
122–125, 126–127; joint optimization, 106–108; and researcher's
values, 119, 124–125; environmental factors, 151–152; criteria,
154; and reductionistic thinking,
153, 161
Rolfing, 75–76

Selection process: in organizations,
17–19, 23–28; and environment,
18; and influence, 18–19; and
leadership, 18–19, 23, 35; criteria,
23–25. *See also* Promotion
Self-acceptance, 53–55
Self-expectation: as research variable,
67–68; and leader behavior, 159
Shadow leaders, 77–78, 158

Social influence: and leadership, 14,
29–31, 87, 91–92. *See also* Influence
Social origins, and success, 26–27
Social science: methodology, xi–xii,
10, 145–149, 153; and values,
148–149
Spines: and leaders, 37–60;
methodology, 59–60
Structure: and linguistics, 89–90;
for research, 10–11, 100
Success, and social origins, 26–27
Succession. *See* Selection process
Surface structure, 89, 91, 100
Systemic problem solving, 130–142;
model for, 130–138; Type III
errors in, 130–131, 132, 134–135;
dialectical process in, 132–134,
135, 138–142; intuition in, 135;
phases in, 135–140; creativity in,
137–138. *See also* Problem
solving
Systems approach, 8–9, 134, 153–154

Technical competence, and leaders,
159
Technology: and joint optimization,
106–108; in high-performing systems, 112–113
Theory: criticism of, 3–4, 7–8; and
leadership strategies, 90–91
Theory X, methodology problems,
118–119
Time horizons, 51–52, 158
Training: criticism of, 5–6; human
relations focus, 5–6; in data
splitting, 52–53
Type III errors: in leadership research, 121–122, 144; in problem
solving, 130–131, 132, 134–135

U.S. Army Research Institute, 155

Values: of researcher, 119, 124–125;
and social science, 148–149